SEX, SOCIETY AND RELATIOSHIPS:

YESTERDAY, TODAY AND TOMORROW

CHARLOTTE SCHWARTZ

SEX, SOCIETY AND RELATIONSHIPS: YESTERDAY, TODAY AND TOMORROW

CHARLOTTE SCHWARTZ

IPBOOKS.net
International Psychoanalytic Books

International Psychoanalytic Books (IPBooks)
New York • IPBooks.net

Book design by Dan Williams

ISBN: 978-1-949093-24-7

Printed in the United States of America

In Memory of my Parents,
Leah and William Slapo.

Table of Contents

Preface

What is infidelity? I suspect that in our minds, we go immediately to some sexual act committed by a married individual—most probably a man, an act of disloyalty to a spouse. Interestingly, the American Heritage Dictionary first, defines infidelity as 'a lack of religious faith,' and secondly as 'sexual betrayal.' I suspect that in our American culture, we almost automatically see infidelity as sexual behavior, not at all connected with religion, but as a sexual act outside of marriage or a committed relationship.

The issues of monogamy and infidelity first drew my attention from patients on the couch. Not especially widespread among my many married men and woman patients, but intriguing from a number of the variations that did occur, from swinging to open marriage. For some of my homosexual patients, cruising or sleeping around in committed relationships became an issue for the other partner. My interest was aroused by the psychological implications for patients, and to the effects of these behaviors on the culture.

Interviews with men and women resulted pretty much in what I had anticipated, pain, rage, feelings of revenge, and distrust. Though the men had a more varied response than the women, there was still a good deal of anger, and hurt. One man rationalized his own behavior of rather frequent sexual interludes with his secretary, and other woman as justification since he had suspected that his wife was unfaithful. Another responded by querying "What is so wrong with an intermittent fling—we are too puritanical in this country—you love your wife—a fling does not effect that love." None of the women were virgins before marriage, but all had expected fidelity except for one woman who relished having affairs and pushed her husband into extramarital sex. Another was involved with swinging but did not easily tolerate her husband's affairs with prostitutes.

While I was concerned with the individual psychological reactions, a parallel interest that seemed to be of equal importance was what was happening in the general society to children and divorced persons, particularly women. Given, the high divorce rate, the number of single parent families, the increase in drugs and alcohol in the young, and rape, especially on the college campuses, it appeared that we were witnessing a host of serious social problems that needed to be understood.

Initially my investigations into the amount of infidelity, divorce rate, age of sexual encounters, and increased emphasis on sex in so many aspects of our life met with a certain recognizable appraisal on my part. But suddenly, the spread of my readings and research opened an unexpected vista that created a sense of shock and even shame. How had I not known of the licentious, and profligate Middle Ages where divorce was more the rule and marriages were short lived, sex was easy at hand, and multiple partners even for the married were not uncommon.

Had the mores of the Victorian era so dominated my thinking that I had not really paid attention to prior history? Even the Greek and Roman history of marriage and sex was more proscribed and restricted by laws than medieval times. The Biblical narratives about adultery were tales of morality and Solomon's seven hundred wives were more a testament to politics than the institution of polygamy. Sexual promiscuity among our ancestors belonged to very ancient history. To read of the Middle Ages as a haven for sexual delights without the restraint of law, and laxity of religion increased my awareness that it was a folly to neglect all of history.

Rethinking of my attitudes toward the sexual revolution of the 1960s and to the sexualized culture of the 21st Century was a priority. It appeared that the 20th and 21st Centuries bore a remarkable resemblance to the sexual mores of the Middle Ages. Did this replay also represent parallel changes in the evolving economic and social conditions in the current society? Or are there merely surface similarities, but profound underlying differences in the nature of the economic forces, the family structure, and the basic social relationships? The role of the Church had begun to exert its strength regarding proper sexual behavior but, it would take many centuries before it could exert its full power over the populace and even the Church body itself. The Church, in spite of its growing power could not stem the tide of infidelity, promiscuity, and prostitution during the Middle Ages. A similar situation exists today, the edicts are strong but the following is weak.

This recognition of the degree of sexual promiscuity of an entire civilized society was quite sobering. If monogamy and fidelity did not quite resonate with our biological disposition, and the so called sexual revolution appeared more an inevitable evolution then what kind of social organization and moral percepts do we require to both satisfy emotional needs, and sexual appetite? What kind of social structure and behavior is necessary that can protect individuals, especially children from the ravages of familial break-downs, dissolution, loneliness, and mental illness? As we study the history of infidelity, sexual behavior, in the context of Church law and secular society, it is possible that we may gain some insights as to where we are and where we need to go.

Introduction

Those who don't remember the past are doomed to repeat it.
—Santayana

The history of love relationships is the most pained—oft repeated—and the least understood. Great novels, Biblical tales, myths, Greek tragedies, and modern Soap Operas remind us of passionate love, lost loves, and love betrayed. In reality, we are forever challenged to suffer the tragedies of love. Desire by nature is fickle and has no morality; we all encounter its power and elusiveness. Victims and victors alike—few escape!

Adultery, infidelity, betrayal—all words that connote a moral and condemnatory meaning—present a difficulty for our discourse, as the preference is to understand not to criticize. Since we are creatures of our culture and have a proscribed vocabulary for these acts, I shall use the terms as they are descriptively valid, and also provide clues to the underlying emotions of people.

The divorce rate in the United States is more than 50 percent and one-third of children live in a single-parent family. The question as to what extent divorce is a result of extramarital affairs is pertinent. That divorce presents difficulties for the individual and society is clearly evident; divorced women have more difficulty than men, and children are reported to fare better in a two-parent family. There has been an increase in divorce after 30 years of marriage. Is there some correlation with infidelity? Couples who live together outside the bounds of marriage have redefined the rules of marriage; if they stray, can we include these arrangements under the rubric of adultery?

To make an inquiry as to what in the act of infidelity causes unhappiness would seem self-evident, but in reality the answers are more complex. A multitude of emotions arise: jealousy, rivalry, competition, rage, and surprisingly, for some a secret pleasure—a voyeuristic delight. The sources from which these emotions derive depend upon a host of characterological factors. The range of psychological conditions is extensive: narcissism, that core of the self that is vulnerable to hurt; jealousy, the need to be the only love object; feelings of insecurity due to a lack of self-worth; fear of abandonment—all have a claim on the emotions. One may also struggle with feelings of subjugation by the lover, and humiliation and shame in face of the community.

Differences between men and women in their sexual behavior and reactions to adultery or infidelity will be explored. Statistics reveal that women in permanent relationships are not so apt as men to have extrasexual affairs: they tend to be more monogamous. To what degree is this determined by the culture, and/or is there a constitutional factor that influences women's behavior in a love relationship? Frequently, we cannot separate the "chicken from the egg" and what we see is such an intertwining of motives that it is difficult to sift through the various factors.

Beginning with the second half of the twentieth century, we have witnessed a radical change in women's sexual behavior. Women are no longer bound by the custom of virginity, and engage in premarital sex almost as frequently as men. The age of sexual intercourse has become younger, occurring around the age of 13. This applies to both females and males. Women, increasingly, view gratifying their passions similarly to men, and the rules of the sexual game apply equally to them. How do we understand the woman who betrays the man? Is she driven by the same desires: a sensuous appetite, power, conquest, retribution, or a search for the perfect love? Constitutionally, are women and men on an equal par in regard to sexual desire, driven by the same forces, and are these of equal intensity?

Do betrayals fundamentally destroy relationships? Are the differences in response between men and women related to economic and educational status? Do racial and class differences affect marriage and adultery?

Understanding patterns of sexual behavior provides insight into the individual's psyche, but also is a clue into the dominant social issues impacting a culture. The question may be raised as to the inevitability of infidelity, given the inherent nature of the sexual instinct. This is especially evident since it has been shown that even good sex in a good marriage does not deter adultery.

A review of the Middle Ages and the Victorian period can

provide some interesting similarities and contrasts to the twenti-eth and twenty-first centuries. It is possible that in viewing these societies the role of monogamy and its counterpart, adultery, will increase our understanding of the biological, psychological, and social forces that influence behavior and social structures.

Indirectly, this study raises the implications of sexual behavior for the whole of society in the twenty-first century. What appears is a wholesale practice of unfettered sexuality, unbound by intimacy or a closer emotional connection to the other. Increasingly, the separation between sex and love forfeits strong emotional bonds between individuals.

To formulate a theory that can encompass biology, individ-ualism, and society, as a way of understanding all the factors that are influential determinants of monogamy, adultery, and sex, is an additional focus of this project.

In respect to the sexual behavior of homosexuals, I will ask similar questions. What role does betrayal play in a long-term relationship, and how does it affect the level of trust and intimacy?

In an ideal world, what would we prefer, monogamy, sexual license, or a little of each?

Chapter One
Rage, Desire and Morality

Morality is the sum of the prejudices of a community.
—Anatole France

Adultery is driven by human passion and punished by the human hand.

On March 10, 1980, Jean Harris, Headmistress of the Madeira School for Girls, walked into her former lover's bedroom and fired five bullets into his body, killing him instantly. Why this murderous act from an intelligent, cultured woman who had much to live for—her children, her career? She was a betrayed woman!

Herman Tarnower, author of the best selling *Scarsdale Diet* book, threw her over for a younger woman. He had been her lover for many years, but, now tired of her, had found himself another mistress.

We can understand her pain, her rage, even her feelings of desperation and desire to win him back, despite his awful treatment. But killing, destroying a man she loved? What occurs in the emotions of a human being that permits this horrendous behavior? Though she claimed that she wanted to commit suicide, and that she tried to get Tarnower to kill her, it was the "Diet Doctor" who was killed. No one is without murderous feelings. The question is, who will act on them and who will control them?

What can we conclude about Jean Harris? Despair at the loss, a sense that the world was bleak and she no longer wanted to live. These feelings would normally lead to depression, inactivity, and a turning inward, a withdrawal from life. But this is not how Jean Harris responded. Betrayal by her lover appeared to evoke some very deep sense of ownership, of entitlement. I want, I must have, and woe to the person who denies me. What an incredible rage! Jean Harris went into action, planned, and acted with premeditation. If she could not have her man, then no other woman would have him. Neither would he have the pleasure of another woman. Killing him, a crime of unbridled, murderous passion, became more important than pursuing her life, finding another lover, or enjoying her family.

All of these alternatives were submerged by her need for revenge, and the destructive wish to get rid of this terrible cancer. Tarnower had denied her what she wanted, what she felt entitled to. There are people, adult, mature, and intelligent, who, despite the outward appearance of good judgment, act in ways that appear inscrutable. Could this very intelligent woman carry within her a very infantile feeling, the demand that every desire or wish be granted? Is it possible that the power of wishes can destroy reason and good judgment? This is not to deny that she was betrayed, but rather to affirm that the roots of response lie in the past, our childhood, and are not governed by present reality. It is normal for the child to regard all persons, and all objects, animate and inanimate, as his /her sole possession. The other person has no existence outside the child's orbit. All needs, all wishes must be gratified. There is hardly a greater rage than the rage of sexual betrayal. As Congreve wrote, "Heaven hath no rage like love to hatred turned/Nor hell a fury like a woman scorned." The anger aroused can be murderous.

The reality that there could be another lover in the life of Tarnower was too devastating for Jean Harris. Uncontrollable emotions have no moral boundaries; unfortunately, they continued to dominate her personality. Thus, when her illusions were shattered, Jean Harris felt as though Herman Tarnower had killed her. By choosing another woman, he was the real murderer, and his death was justified by her belief that he too had killed, "an eye for a eye, a tooth for a tooth!"

Amy Fisher rang the bell of her lover's home, and blasted his wife's face with gunshot. Fisher did not try to kill her lover, but his wife. Strange as it may seem, the wife was seen as Amy's victimizer, and not the reverse. Why did she try to kill the innocent wife and not her guilty lover?

Amy Fisher, in contrast to Jean Harris, did not get rid of her man. She turned on her rival and tried to destroy her. She did not blame the unfaithful lover, but rather his wife, whom she regarded as very powerful. For Fisher, Mrs. Buttafuoco was the rival!

Amy Fisher became the American Hera, the Greek goddess who sought revenge on the women with whom Jupiter fornicated. Often, hatred of the rival is greater than rage at the unfaithful lover. Envy of Joey Buttafuoco's wife was the motivating force behind Amy Fisher's actions. In her mind, Amy Fisher had constructed a triangle. Joey was hers, and his wife was the rival trying to take him away. Her desires blinded her ability to understand the reality of the situation; the wife, the other woman, was the thief, not Amy. Underlying this envy of the wife and jealousy lay an equally destructive force, that of greed. Amy wanted what the wife had. She felt entitled to have him. No one has any rights in comparison to one's own desires. Thus, Amy Fisher felt perfectly justified in trying to get rid of Mrs. Buttafuoco.

Western literature and history are rife with betrayal, murder, and pain. Medea, betrayed by Jason, killed their children; Henry VIII, the consummate whorer, was a killer of his wives; and Anna Karenina, Dostoevsky's fictional character, also betrayed by her lover, committed suicide. The list is endless

Men also have been driven by murderous rages to kill the women whom they think have betrayed them. Shakespeare's great play *Othello* brings to life the murderous jealousies of men. Othello, a great general and war hero, is easily persuaded of his wife's supposed infidelity and kills her despite her innocence. O.J. Simpson, the American football hero stood trial for shooting his ex-wife and younger boyfriend. Though he was acquitted, the world deemed him guilty.

We may well ask: what drives some to kill and others who endure infidelity to stay or walk away? Every betrayed person will respond according to his/ her temperament and character. Fear, rage, love, economic dependence, custom, endurance, and law all influence individual responses to infidelity. Some leave the marriage or relationship immediately; others give numerous chances, and there are those who in an act of revenge become unfaithful, while others suffer in silence. Killing an unfaithful lover is not out of the realm of human possibilities. The song "Frankie and Johnny" sums it up: "He was my man but I did him in—" Yet most betrayed persons do not kill their lovers. Morality, that social arbiter, has instilled a high sense of the value of human life.

Crimes of passion, although understood and even pitied, do not escape the hand of justice.

Differences Between Men and Women in their Attitudes and Behaviors with Infidelity

As we examine the various responses to adultery and unfaithfulness, we encounter a rather interesting observation regarding men and women. What emerged in the research was a decided difference in their attitudes toward faithfulness and unfaithfulness. (The National Institute of Mental Health, 3–26–2016). Research revealed that women were more tolerant of men's infidelity than men were of women's infidelity. Women appeared more distressed by the emotional involvement and intimacy with another woman than by the sexual encounter. Men appeared to react with less distress and greater erotic arousal to the idea of their wives' unfaithfulness with other women, but were very distressed by an affair with the opposite sex. Women seemed to react more negatively to the idea of their partner's engaging in sex with another man, and showed less distress at betrayal with the opposite sex. Women indicated a greater need for emotional connection while men tended to react more negatively to sexual infidelity than to emotional infidelity.

Ken was enraged—how could she! His estranged wife, whom he had left after 12 years of marriage, had an affair. He was livid; he fumed; he was devastated. It did not matter that he no longer loved her, felt bored with her. She had betrayed him. Nor did it matter that in reality he had had numerous affairs throughout the marriage. His wife knew of his affairs; this did not bother him, but how dare she sleep with another man so soon after the separation; maybe she had slept with him before! "He would never go back to her after what she had done."

An interesting contradiction arises between reality and emotion, and between intelligence and emotion. Betrayal looms large in the emotional lives of women and men. The most frequent cause of wife-beating and killing is infidelity. Female killing of males is also, due in large part to infidelity. We may well argue that infidelity is simply the symptom of a bad or difficult relationship, especially the sexual relationship between the couple. If the relationships were really good, we would have very little infidelity. This turns out to be false, for in many very good marriages, where the sexual relationship is very satisfying, acts of infidelity still occur.

Studies show that between 1960 and 1980 there has been an increase in the number of husbands who confess to their wives that they have been unfaithful. Interestingly, the same is not true for women. Women tend to keep a secret better than their husbands. That men confess may be due to the fact that women are more confrontational, and glean the truth more adeptly. Since women have become more financially independent, they are less frightened of confronting the truth. Remember that infidelity is the third highest cause of divorce, and instigated most frequently by women. (Divorce, from Wikipedia, the free encyclopedia, 1/27/16).

Why women hold secrets better, and do not feel obligated to confess, is interesting. Perhaps men do not wish to know of the infidelity; they cannot believe that they have been betrayed, cuckolded: denial is a good protective device against wounded self-esteem. Men seem to be more easily wounded in losing the competitive battle with other men, especially in relationships with women. Men's intolerance of infidelity is experienced as a loss of love and lack of empowerment. Denial is a good protection, and thus they usually do not confront the partner; they don't even suspect. Men report a much higher rate of emotional and sexual satisfaction in marriage. They appear more oblivious to the unhappiness of their partners, or simply to the fact that a loving wife can also want others. In a sense, ignorance is bliss. Some writers claim that a hypocritical stance is the best way to preserve a marriage. It is not necessary to flaunt all behaviors—a momentary fling or a discreet tryst—in the partner's face. Love and understanding can co-exist with an act of infidelity.

Linda and Bob had an open marriage. Each had affairs and each knew when and with whom the other slept. Then Linda committed the ultimate sin in his mind. She had an affair with a friend of theirs and did not tell Bob about it; a mutual friend told him. Bob felt betrayed and he left her, breaking up the marriage after 15 years.

Why was Ken so distraught? How was it that he could be unfaithful throughout the marriage, and yet be so distraught at the thought of his wife's having an affair, though they were separated? Why did Bob feel betrayed when Linda had an affair and didn't tell him? Did Bob ever have affairs and not tell Linda? Yes! What is the meaning of this double standard? I can, but she can't! It is not a logical reaction, but one stemming from pure emotion. As a generality, men have more difficulty in handling unfaithfulness by their wives: an interesting psychological factor, since, men are more unfaithful than women.

What, exactly, in the adulterous act is so distressing to the other? How does adultery injure one's self-esteem? Does it represent a rivalry in which you have lost the battle; does it arouse uncomfortable feelings of envy, a feeling of rejection, and a loss of basic trust in one's partner? Why should these acts of adultery lead to a disruption of family life, loss of structure for children, rejection of someone you still love, and often, for the woman, economic distress? Some answers may lie in the wish for exclusivity, the need to be the sole love object. Are these desires for exclusivity, to have total love and total attention, adaptive emotions for the mature mind? These are not conscious feelings, but are inherent in the nature and demands of our early development that are not easily dispelled. The failure to socialize these wishes very early in life interferes with our adult judgments and behavior. Thus, there exists the contradiction between our desires to have whatever we want, many sexual partners, many loves, and the wish to be the only one desired. Emotions play tricks with reality.

Chapter Two
Why Sex

Throughout history, sex and aggression appear to be the main staples of human experience. No matter how the culture changes, where people live, or the nature of their economic activity, they are perpetually dealing with their sexuality and desire to kill. Sex provides great pleasure, but also despair. Killing gives more distress, yet, hard to believe, sometimes pleasure.

Let us ask what may seem an odd, and rather obvious question: why sex, why are we humans desirous of sex? We all assume, the basic purpose is to reproduce, to have offspring, in order to perpetuate the human race. Of course, sex is pleasurable and thus, aside from increasing humanity, we gain some personal delight. Yet, there is such a thing in nature, as asexual reproduction; certain plants and animals can procreate by themselves (Ridley, 1993). There is no need for a partner. The genetic makeup is simply given to the next generation, no complicated involvement with another. So why has sex with a mate developed for most animals, and all humans? Darwin (1859) whose early work *On the Origins of the Species* indicated that "separation of the sexes in plant life would be more advantageous due to the separation of labour," and " individuals with this tendency more and more increased would be continually favoured or selected. . . ." (p.169). Current geneticists support a theory called "The Red Queen" theory that originated with Ridley (1993), and posited the idea that to ensure survival against disease and early death a two-person couplet, man and woman, provided the best protection for the organism against deadly viruses and parasites. The Red Queen theory is not yet provable but is maintained as the most efficient logical explanation as to why the two-partner system developed, despite the fact that in numerous ways asexual reproduction is more efficient. A second theory proposed that "heterozygotes" also provide better protection against disease than "homozygotes": that is, when two separate and different chromosomal (phenotypic genes) unite, they offer more protection against deadly disease. A third explanation, the theory of "Mixability," (Livant, Papadimitriou, Dushoff, and Feldman, 2007) asserted that even with bad genes or harmful mutations sexual genes are more flexible than asexual genes. This makes possible a better adjustment to the environment that is ever-changing. Therefore, copulation, a function of our biological makeup, and the drive for sexual union between a male and a female are inherent in our genetic structure. Ridley (1993) further indicated that aspects of the drive to reproduce has within it psychological elements of competition, this in order to find the youngest and prettiest mate for the male. Thus, to ensure the survival of the best genes, and to continue reproducing, the male competes, even at times, putting himself in danger. Youth and beauty signify the healthiest of the genetic pool and offer greater reproductive potential. This competition to secure the best of mates, especially for the male, would appear to underlie their aggressive behavior. He has indicated that males are more aggressive than females because the human female's genetic structure produces a more nurturing role in caring for the young, and therefore renders her less driven to dangerous behaviors. The consequence of this mode of genetically-driven was that the competitive, aggressive male's fighting for the younger, prettier women had impacted the psychological behavior of male and female sexuality. Ridley had argued for the role of nature over nurture, though he certainly gave credit to the environment and to the culture. His thesis maintained that nature was the dominant feature in the programming of sexuality. While various cultures and the individual environment can define the outer manifestations of sexuality, its basic qualities, such as passive or aggressive acts, rivalry, exhibitionism, masculinity and femininity, are better defined by an underlying genetic construct that functions to perpetuate the fittest of the human gene.

Helen Fisher (2004), author and researcher on sex and marriage, has provided some interesting data for our theories of human genes that influence sex and love. Fisher maintained that the chemicals dopamine, serotonin, testosterone, and estrogen all play a role in sexual arousal. As chemical neurotransmitters in the brain, they influence both personality types and sexual behavior. She indicated that, aside from the part of male-female intercourse in reproduction, sex plays an important role in physical health; it reduces the risk of heart disease, improves overall fitness, contributes to weight loss, reduces pain, the frequency of colds and flu, and improves bladder control. In women, sex notably reduces depression and rejuvenates women's menstrual cycle. For men, the chemicals dopamine and norepinephrine in the seminal fluid relieve stress and provide energy. An important psychological finding in genetic determinants is the role which certain chemicals, such as oxytocin, play in human attachment and romantic passion.

In psychological terms, we translate this into the manner in which innate drives stimulate both physical and emotional desire. Even in casual sex, hormones can stimulate passion and deep feelings of attachment. At the same time, certain hormones increase sexual desire and are responsible for a "more varied sexual experience" (Fisher, p.128).

Yet there appears to be a contradiction between the emotions of attachment, presumably to one person, and varied sexual experiences with others that do not result in an attachment. For the purposes of this exploration of infidelity, we wish to raise the issue: is attachment an emotion that is possible to maintain with numerous persons in sexual encounters? Fisher (1992) has pointed out that men tend to fall in love more frequently than women, and appear to fall in love or become attached even in a "one night stand." Women, even in causal one-night sexual encounters, are really searching for attachment, while men tend to have more casual sex without attachments. There are many contradictory results both in the studies and in human behavior. Men want more casual sex, but become attached too easily, while women have causal sex, but want attachment. Are these seeming contradictions due to different genetic or chemical traits that run counter to psychological and emotional needs, or are the contradictions a result of culture, which develops at times in a way that is in opposition to our more basic psychological needs? Fisher (2004) addressed the role of dopamine in maintaining a strong love attachment concurrent with great passion, lust, and falling in love. Men are also capable of a short attention span and are able to move to the next mate with equal passion. She equates this with the biological need to reproduce. (pp. 72–76). Thus, our frequent looking askance at the fickle, and particularly, the roving Romeo, needs to be reappraised. If genetics are responsible for shifting love allegiances, and the chemicals dopamine, testosterone, and possibly norepinephrine play a significant role in sexual arousal, then the battle is not only psychological and moral, but we are fighting basic biology.

The evolutionists tend to regard infidelity as a consequence of the procreative forces in our genetic makeup. The sexual drive is stimulated by a series of coordinated impulses that are generated from various genes. Man is programmed by evolution to replenish the species, to reproduce. He can inseminate many females in a day, many more in a week, and so on. The female is programmed to gestate for nine months, and generally produces one child. The male sperm is facile, searching out numerous ova; the female can handle only one pregnancy at a time, despite the fact that she may have copulated with a number of men in succession. There is a genetic and constitutional difference between the male and the female. The male role is to spread his sperm to many females, while the woman can ovulate with only one male's sperm, the choicest of them. She is highly selective, while the male is more indiscriminate. The logical assumption from these facts is to conclude that infidelity is rooted in biology, driven by the need to spread the male's sperm and to constantly replenish the population.

Michel Foucault (1978), the noted cultural philosopher, presents us with a very different mode of conceptualization. Sexuality, he states, is the prisoner of society. The economic and political forces of societies exercise fundamental control of our sexual bodies. Various periods in history, from Feudal times and the Renaissance, to modern times, may show different behavioral characteristics in regard to sexuality, morality and promiscuity, but essentially he claims that these differences and even samenesses reflect the ideology of the dominant ruling class. The laws, mores, and attitudes regarding sex, or what Foucault refers to as "the body," are determined by the dominant mode of production, that is, the work of people whose bodies are used to meet the needs of this class. Therefore, in Foucault's lexicon, sexuality, though based upon biology, is given its particular expression by society, and controlled not by the individual or the family, but by the dominant members of a society who determine the mode of the culture.

Thus, Foucault adds another dimension to the nurture-nature argument by introducing the power of economic and political forces in determining sexual behavior. Emotions, the mental representation of biology, would, in his conceptualization, bear primarily the imprint of organized social forces.

Since I place emotions within the mind/body spectrum, that is, a biological framework from which to view sexuality, our queries about sexuality become even more complex. Emotions give rise to mental ideas in the brain, and these ideas also result in physical, and psychologically determined behaviors. (Vygotsky, 1954) As emotions bear the imprint of hormonal activity, we are constantly torn between explanations from psychology, biology, and the influence of environment.

Sigmund Freud, one of the great geniuses of the ninetieth and twentieth centuries, and the founder of psychoanalysis, gave the title "instinct" to sexual activity. He claimed that instinct "appears to us as a concept on the frontier between the mental and the somatic, as the psychical representative of the stimuli originating from within the organism and reaching the mind . . ." (Freud, 1915, 121–122). In current terminology, we would regard an instinct as an inborn element coded in the DNA that in humans, as opposed to many animals, prescribes not a specific activity, but rather a generalized pattern of activity that contains certain intrinsic qualities that are embedded in the genes. Thus, as the code for language is not specific to a particular language, but rather to languages in general, determined by the environment, the instincts for sex and aggression are equally coded. Thus, the sexual instinct has a generalized quality, related primarily to reproduction through sexual union, but is also understood as a force to which we have given the name *libido,* which influences love, attachment, understanding, and social connection. The nature of the instinct's pressure upon the mind and its effect upon the body has been a problem to be solved for most of civilization's developmental history. Psychology, as a field of study of human mental functioning, was introduced into our lexicon as a bridge of study between body and mind and environment. Therefore, an issue that continues to perplex us is how much of the culture harmonizes with our biological and psychological makeup, and how much does culture accentuate various individual elements of biology?

The Hebrew Bible and the Ten Commandments, written down in approximately the sixth century BCE, was already a testament to what is inherent in human nature and evident in human behavior. The two commandments "Thou Shall Not Kill" and "Thou Shalt Not Covet Thy Neighbors Wife" (thou shalt not commit adultery) are rules that civilization must try to uphold on a daily basis (Yalom, 2001). These two commandments bears witness to the fact that unfettered sexuality and aggression posed danger to the wellbeing of society and the person; therefore, laws to rein in these two instincts were established. With the passage of time, certain strictures, social, legal, and religious, arose for the protection of organized civilization. And yet, with all our laws both legal and religious, we cannot contain killing, adultery, and promiscuity.

Another dilemma in understanding the various tributaries of the sexual drive is why rape occurs, and what place does it have in our sexual genetic structure? Is rape a cultural misuse of our basic instincts? Some theorists concerned with evolutionary sociobiology suggest that rape serves an evolutionary purpose, that of survival of the fittest. Much of the research has been with animals and subsequently applied to human behavior. They feel that rape resulted from a reproductive strategy that was motivated by the genetic structure in animals, and also humans (Thiessen & Thiessen 1985). Recognition is given to the idea that though certain behaviors are inherent, the interaction between genetic structures and environment plays a significant role and that this interaction could influence and modify biologically driven behaviors. It is still considered that the basic impulse for rape lay in our long evolutionary pattern of "reproductive adaptability." Others (Tobach, Schwendinger, and Schwendinger, 1985) have questioned the supposition as to the applicability of transferring observations from animal behavior to humans, and secondly, the theoretical basis for divining a genetic basis for rape. Further, they question the basic premise as to whether rape, even in the animal kingdom, was productive for reproductive capacities. They found that a statistical evaluation of rapists and their victims regarding reproduction showed a very limited capacity by the rapist to reproduce, and a very limited pregnancy rate among the victims. It appears that rapists often have difficulties in ejaculation, and generally poor performance in the sexual act. Their results indicate that the rapist is not driven by the evolutionary drive for reproduction.

Yet, as we look backwards in history, we observe that every century has witnessed vivid pictures of indiscriminate rape of women, young girls, and young boys. Laws of Consent were established as late or early as 1275 CE, to protect young girls from rape and sexual predators. The age of consent varied according to the country from the age of 10—16, and later rose to the age of 18. At a somewhat later period boys were also included in the Laws of Consent, in order to protect them from homosexual abuse or from older women. Unfortunately, the history of rape appears as ancient as that of mankind.

The stories of King Arthur's court and its gallant knights with their courtly love of women are rife with tales of who and when it is permissible to rape. The custom permitted the knight to easily rape the woman of the field, and, with somewhat more hesitancy, permission was also given to him to take by force the woman of the court. In our time, we observe rape on college campuses and in war-torn countries; even in the name of religious fervor, rape runs rampant. Twenty two percent of imprisoned rapists in the United States are married, a surprising number when the issue is not simply the presence of a sexual partner.

Just as we are concerned with the whys of infidelity and adultery, rape comes under the same umbrella. I am alluding to the factor of sexual and aggressive instincts and their interplay with psychology and culture. The force of the drives are there, and the history of civilization has been plagued by the destructive actions of these two instincts, the need to gratify them, to give pleasure, and most important, to ensure the survival of the human race. Civilization finds itself in a continuous dilemma between the forces of instinct, the forces of psychology, and the laws of morality. There is a fight between raw biology and the human need for mental peace; it is not simply survival of the body, but the survival of a healthy human mind, equilibrium within the emotions, and the safety of society.

From procreation to love, to marriage, adultery, infidelity, social structure, and even war, we can observe the rather circuitous path of the sexual instinct, and thus the rule of biology in spite of the power of environment.

Chapter Three
Monogamy and Sexual Desire

In the schema of human existence, monogamy is a fairly new development. Paleoanthropologists estimate that monogamy had its onset about ten thousand to twenty thousand years ago. (Lovejoy, 1981). Considering that human development began over 1.8 million years ago, with *Homo habilis*, and that the ancestor of modern man is estimated to have existed about 400, 000 thousand years ago, monogamy is in its early childhood. One theory regarding pair-bonding states that in order to protect the young and the mother, pairing was a necessary development and thus explained the development of monogamy. Promiscuous behavior, the tormentor of monogamy, provides support for a second theory, that man is driven to spread his seed and therefore, increase the genetic pool by inseminating as many females as possible. Lovejoy (1981) claimed that pair-bonding and a rudimentary family unit existed during the time of *Homo erectus*. This bipedal male was able to care for mother and child by bringing food to this unit, thus ensuring a higher survival rate. It is possible that this early pairing resembled a monogamous unit. Though others have suggested that early man and woman were not monogamous, but rather polygamous, encompassing one male and multiple women. Evidently, the issue of monogamy, polygamy, and promiscuity among the human hominids has been a source of much inquiry and many theories. Further, attempts have been made to draw parallels with the animal kingdom in order to see if monogamy is a socially learned behavior or is inherent in our genetic structure. Various studies indicate that 30% of primates are monogamous while only 3% of all mammals are monogamous. From these statistical reports, it is difficult to draw an analogy from animal to human behavior.

The first recording of a relationship between a man and a woman was in Mesopotamia in 2350 BCE. The Bible has repeated references to monogamy and adultery, and the edict that "Thou shalt not covet thy neighbor's wife" indicates that the state of monogamy was well established within the annals of history. This not only tells us about the legitimate role that monogamy played in the organization of society, but also indicates that its laws were frequently breached.

Egyptian society was also noted for the rule of monogamy, particularly among the commoner class. For people of nobility and royalty, a different set of marriage customs applied. A pharaoh married his first wife, the queen, and then could take a number of minor wives. Divorce was easy to attain, yet if a woman committed adultery it could result in punishment; burning or stoning were common methods utilized for this act. It is questionable if the same punishments were applied to men. The early Greek and Roman societies also had strict laws governing marriage, monogamy, and adultery. Still, concubines and sex with slaves or prostitutes were permitted to the male.(Scheidel, 2008).

Most theories regard monogamy not as a genetic or a biologically determined mode of behavior, but as evolving from a long history of social development. Scheidel (2008) uses the term SIUM, "socially imposed universal monogamy," as a means of citing the evolution of social mores. Infidelity and adultery, terms that can only be understood in relationship to monogamy, would then appear as actions determined by social conditions. Yet it is possible to consider that these two behaviors, aside from the influence of the social environment, may be propelled by an underlying genetic factor, as Ryder suggests in his Red Queen theories. The sexual instinct that is driven by genetics to spawn the seed in as many females as possible pushes the male toward many sexual partners. The female is also a pawn of nature; fundamentally she is driven to find the choicest of sperm, and thus mating with many men is biologically determined. That statistics show that men are far more unfaithful, more roving then women, does not diminish the role of genetic influences in the woman. Finding the best mate may also underlie man's drive for monogamy, in order to secure his sperm permanently. Species and individuals, male and female, are all governed by different genetic structures and characteristics. Testosterone, a sexual hormone, is much higher in the male and undoubtedly contributes to his higher level of infidelity. Further, the male is not hindered by the long period of pregnancy, nursing, or menstruation. The wax and wane of the female sexual drive naturally plays havoc with a higher degree of sexual desire in the male (Fisher, 2004, 1992).

It is not possible to discuss the development of monogamy

without first recognizing early man's understanding of the role of humans in reproduction. Some occurrence of significant magnitude had to have changed the course of man's cognitive development and his knowledge of sexuality. Theories indicate that our early ancestors had no concept of human reproduction. Their first beliefs stemmed from animistic and supernatural concepts. The modern version of the stork had its precedents in various bird stories that brought the baby to the mother, or else incubated the fetus within the woman. Women were thought to function as a container; their role in producing an ovum came gradually. When it was recognized that women had a role in reproduction, they were looked upon with great admiration, and were elevated to a lofty status. Women were transformed into Goddesses of Fertility, and many rights were conveyed to them. Gradually, the male role was recognized: he was the fertilizer, the giver of life, and the woman was again judged as merely the container. Undoubtedly, this cognitive view, in addition to changing economic and social conditions, led to the increased power of the male.

Families in the Distant Past
and Changing Economic Conditions

To travel even a greater distance into the past, the Stone Age, that ended somewhere between 6000 and 2000 BCE, we will find that in the later Paleolithic period, families were loosely organized around groups of about thirty people with several male leaders. Loosely bound relationships among men and women were domi-nant in this Hunter-Gatherer period, essentially a nomadic society. Food and care of young and old rested with the entire group; even nursing was distributed among the various women. The society was essentially egalitarian, and all shared in the group's resources. That there were frequent changes of sexual partners is supported by found remnants of DNA in children of the same groupings or family units. Within the group bound by the basic exigencies of life, there was no need for exclusive ownership of individuals or property. The psychology of these people would appear to have been shaped by the nature of their economic existence. The sense of power or self-worth, especially for the male, rested in his ability to hunt, while for the female, who labored as the gatherer, the sense of self also lay in her ability to exploit nature, to take what was already grown (Hunter-Gatherers Wikipedia).

As societies developed and populations increased, the usual methods of providing food and necessities for living were no longer adequate; hunting and gathering could not be sustained as a viable economic system. A new mode of production developed, first pastoral, followed by an agricultural economy that required a stationary work force. Men became tillers of the soil, and though women helped with certain aspects of farming, increasingly their role changed from outside to inside. The women became the homemakers and the sole caretakers of children. These changes in work tasks and general economics impacted the nature of male and female relationships. Women, once equal to men, found themselves in a more dependent position. Private ownership of property became the new norm, as communal ownership no longer met the needs of this new social and economic organization. The male assumed lordship over home and hearth, and though women ruled inside the home, their social role was diminished in power. Increasingly, women and children were viewed as possessions, as part of accumulated wealth; the wealthier the male became, the more powerful he was viewed. He was no longer the hunter of wild animals, but a man of property and material possessions. Marriage and monogamy as a legal system solidified the social position of the male. Women increasingly became both economically and psychologically part of men's accumulated wealth. Individual care and love by a wife bolstered the male's self esteem, and provided a reliable source of sex and progeny. This too enhanced his productivity, and increased his power ("The Invisible Sex," Wikipedia 2007).

From this system of private ownership, new concepts arose regarding the place of inheritance within the family. Previously, the idea of inheritance had little meaning, since property was held in common. Now, in conjunction with private ownership, inheritance became an important part of individual and family power. The first-born male child was deemed the successor to his father. Subsequently, he became more powerful than his mother and sisters. Inheritance by the eldest son as the next head of the household presents an interesting psychological phenomena. Not only is the son an extension of the father, the powerful male, but, through him, the father maintained a sense of immortality. Humans do not give up life easily, as the history of burial rites indicate. As the woman in most cultures continued under the control of the son, her subsidiary position was maintained. In this context, the son too, had a vested interest in maintaining chastity for the woman. A chaste mother protects the filial relationship to the father and guarantees an inheritance that could be jeopardized by an unfaithful mother. Not only individuals, but an entire society organized on the basis of private property, had a vested interest in maintaining monogamy and condemning adultery. That adultery was also viewed askance for the male arose from the recognition that doubts as to the paternity of the son jeopardized the heirs' rights of inheritance. A bastard son could be at a disadvantage; so could a cuckolded man whose private property, *i.e.,* his children, were in doubt. As lords and a ruling aristocracy began to dominate in the new social order, we observe that the once equal man, the hunter, increasingly became a class of peasants, serfs, and work- ers. Monogamy, in this new economic and political landscape, assumed new purposes. Beyond protection of the young and the mother, and guaranteeing the male's genetic pool, it became im- portant to have a stabilized family unit in order to maintain social cohesion, and, most important, the protection of property rights. Further, as fighting among groups, fiefdoms, war-lords, and states and countries became the norm, marriage and monogamy was recognized as a more efficient means for control of the populace, especially the men. Lukas and Clutton-Brock (2013) developed a theory of monogamy that pointed to "location" and "supply." They indicate that a lower density of women made monogamy a more efficacious method for personal and sexual gratification. Monogamy for warriors also aided in establishing a cohesive army, thus limiting the search for women and enabling more focus on fighting and loyalty to the lord.

No one factor stands alone in the development of monogamy. Equal weight must be given to economic, intellectual, social, and psychological understandings.

Marriage protected children and provided the male with a secure relationship and viable heirs. Through monogamy, women were ensured protection against the hazards of life, and were provided with permanent security for themselves and their children. A new and different psychology developed under this system of paired bonding with marriage and monogamy. This shift from primarily a group or tribal attachment to a smaller family unit solidified the relationship between the individual male and female, and to their genetic children. Thus, monogamy was birthed.

Attachment, an emotion that has the capacity to bind people together and even to create ties to other animate life, and to the inanimate, derives from a specific aspect of the sexual instinct. Sexuality, aside from its basic reproductive drives, also inherently provides the capacity for love, understanding, sympathy, kindness, and identification with another. Society does not create sexuality; its biological roots are universal, but culture can define the forms, the mode of expression, and even define who and how to love. To accept the idea that love is a constituent of sex dethrones the lofty idealism that surrounds love. Religions are especially egregious in this regard, and sexuality has often been debased even within the marriage bed. Thus, to understand monogamy in its historical development, we need to study the particular contours in each social system, and the mode by which rules and moral precepts intertwine with the sexual drive.

Contradictory pulls in the sexual instinct are factors that each society, each system of religion, each economic and political era must also understand, and take into consideration when establishing edicts and modes of behavior. Sex has the capacity to bind individuals, and at the same time this same instinct has a wandering quality. It appears to pull the individual toward other sexual objects. The primary explanation that we have already discussed indicated that the sex drive is genetically wired to serve the goals of reproduction, and it is this wiring that is also responsible for our attraction to different sexual beings, to reproduce as much as possible. This would explain the male's wandering eye. Furthermore, to ensure the survival of the fittest, men and women search out sexual partners who will protect and enhance the human race genetically. That biology and psychology are the culprits when infidelity raises its unpretty head does not always satisfy the wish for a definitive answer. Perhaps at best we can only claim that biology, psychology, and society coalesce at different stages in the history of civilization and take on different dimensions and dress. One or the other, or many—the instincts, sex or aggression, or a coalescence of the two; social factors, religion, legal restrictions, or permissiveness may also become the dominant factors. Psychology, a factor of mind and emotions, responds to changes in social customs and may, more or less, be influenced by culture, depending to what degree society can gratify fundamental emotional needs. Biology, too, can succumb to the repressions of society, but only so far. At times, sexuality runs amok and plays havoc with personal and social realities, especially basic survival needs of women and children. Monogamy rests upon a slippery slope, always subject to the forces of culture and at the mercy of biology.

Chapter Four
A History of Adultery

In our prehistory, women and men had numerous sexual partners (Scheidel, 2008). There was mating as often as desired. Adultery had no meaning prior to the development of the institution of marriage. Even as society became more organized, free sexual relationships continued to exist. This applied to all types of relationships, the committed or bonded, loose associations, or casual encounters. Prohibitions were few in this early pristine culture where man roamed freely.

Scheidel's (2008) studies of monogamy and adultery encompass a massive amount of material that covers thousands of years of Eurasian, African and American cultures. He found that even in later centuries, when monogamy had been established as a fairly uniform system, that among certain groups of American Indians, women and men continued to mate freely, and husbands and wives were exchanged at frequent intervals. In some groups, mates could be exchanged daily. There were tribes in Africa that engaged in uninhibited sexual activity, freely exchanging partners, pre- or post-marriage. Women in these societies had sexual rights equal to those of men, and from outward appearances were as fickle and lustful as the men.

We may well ponder what the mindset was of the people in these ancient or prehistoric societies that led them to follow their sexual desire with so many different partners. Did the shifts from permissive to more stringent rules occur in a linear pattern, or did the various cultures diverge within the same time period, some more permissive, others more restrictive? Scheidel (2008) indicates that Imperial State formation was conducive to the growth of harems for rulers while "polygyn [polygamy, my insertion] was much more limited in sub-elite circles". (p.5) Monogamy and polygamy often existed side by side. As populations increased together with the rise of large state formations, monogamy appeared as a more viable manner in which to regulate the population and the society. The Old Testament, written down about the sixth century BCE, already had prohibitions against adultery. The Book of *Numbers* (8:21) not only prohibits adultery but, is quite explicit in delineating punishment for the "crime." The woman was regarded as primarily the guilty partner, and she was to be flogged and killed. Thus, it was already evident that marriage and monogamy were sacred, and adultery was considered a threat to the organization of society.

Law and Adultery

It should come as no surprise that the laws against adultery were applied most stringently to women. Surprisingly, the twenty-first century is still witness to punishments by death for the crime of adultery. Millions of women in Muslim countries continue to live under the subjugation of anti-adultery laws (*Quran*). They are stoned to death, hanged, or chased out of the community, as pariahs, unwelcome by all. This barbarism has a long history. Punishment by death was a common practice. Men sometimes suffered the consequences of adultery, and they too were punished or killed, though, generally, there was a more permissive attitude regarding men's adulterous behavior. Unfortunately, women were designated as the seductresses, the betrayers of morals. By the twentieth century, most western societies had removed legal sanctions against women who are unfaithful to their husbands, though in the United States of America, 23 states still have laws against adultery for both men and women. Pejorative terms such as *whore* and *slut* continue to plague women's good name while men escape the verbal condemnation. The history of adultery is essentially a history of double standards. It also is a history that has attempted to control human sexuality, particularly the female's sexuality.

Clearly, adultery appeared dangerous to our ancestors, so much a threat to society that the seventh commandment declares "That Thou Shalt Not Covet Thy Neighbor's Wife." It is, certainly, significant that the prohibition against adultery had been included in the Ten Commandments, laws that were believed to emanate from God. Obviously, adultery, especially on the part of the woman, appeared to threaten both the social fabric of the society and the psychological wellbeing of people. Yet, men could escape the prohibition by acquiring handmaidens, second wives, and concubines. A woman, however, was restricted to one husband whom she shared with others. Though women appeared to accept this social order, we observe that these relationships were fraught with rivalries and jealousies as recorded in the Biblical tale of Rachel and Leah, Jacob's two wives. And Sarah, the most prominent of our early forebears, orders Abraham to send away Hagar, her handmaiden, with her son Ishmael, fathered by Abraham, into the desert because she perceives them as threats to her own power and to Isaac's lineage.

Virginity

In the annals of history, the laws against adultery rarely existed without a parallel attitude toward virginity. To think of virginity is to think of the female, hardly ever the male. The history of virginity is as complicated as the history of adultery. Among the Persians, virginity was required for both sexes; the Sumerians required virginity only in the female, and the Hebrews looked away when the male strayed. The female who lost her virginity prior to marriage was stoned to death. (Scheidel, 2008)

There were some cultures (Scheidel, 2008) where virginity was not at a premium. Russia, Tibet, and Babylon considered virginity in the woman a negative quality. The major disgrace for a woman was sterility and thus it was important to know before marriage that a woman could bear children. Virgin women were regarded with suspicion and suspected of having some deficiency. Frequently, they were considered undesirable marriage partners.

In the distant annals of history, (Scheidel, 2008) societies developed a more unified attitude toward virginity, adultery, and free sexual intercourse. Monogamy, virginity, and chastity took on a virtuous aura, and became increasingly infused with religious doctrine and secular laws (fourteenth to seventeenth centuries). The laws against adultery, and insistence on virginity, institutionalized society's belief that unbridled sex would result in behaviors detrimental to both individuals and the social order. There were not only laws against adultery, but also laws about sexual behavior in general. Masturbation, according to the Bible, was considered a crime and punishable by death. In Persian society, masturbation was punishable by flogging. Unmarried women who had sexual relations were chased out of the community or put to death. Again, we note that women who strayed sexually were treated far more harshly than men.

As we have already pointed out, women's chastity became important legally in order to ensure the legitimacy of the male's paternity. Further, as the knowledge of the human role in reproduction began to impact and dispel supernatural beliefs, the sexual and emotional relationships between individuals became more important. Sexual attraction led to emotional union, even if it was only of short duration. The increased awareness that the sexual union between the male and female resulted in pregnancy resulted in strengthened emotional bonds. Further, the realization that they created a child together had to contribute to a sense of personal power and high self-regard. Adultery by either undermined these internal feelings of personal power. For the male, the damage was even greater, for adultery challenged his assumptions regarding his paternity. As society changed from the hunter-gatherer mode to small familial units and private ownership, not only of material property but human property, monogamy and adultery affected the individual psychology. Competition among men was no longer primarily about physical strength and hunting skills, but in attaining young and beautiful women who would add to their wealth by bearing children. Adultery by the man also caused injury by interfering with another man's property, *i.e.*, the legitimacy of his heirs. This largely accounts for punishment of the male in many societies. Economic and social reasons account for the application of laws against adultery; but increasingly, as the culture changes, psychological aspects of human behavior and interactions play an equally important role.

Chapter Five
The Middle Ages

I have selected the Middle Ages as a focal point to examine sexual behaviors and infidelities within the parameters of a developed society that had already begun to display some social and economic characteristics that would resonate in the later twentieth and twenty-first centuries. As a historical precursor, this period presented an interesting prototype for future generations. What is reflected in our current era are similar unrepressed sexual behaviors, the edicts of religious and legal authorities, and the contradictions between belief and behavior. The increasingly powerful religious organization, the Catholic Church, with its edicts against unfettered sexuality, even within the marriage bed, had its origins in this period. The differences between the Middle Ages and the present lie in the familial, social, and economic organization of a rural society versus our current highly industrialized, urban society. ("Middle Ages," *The Free Encyclopedia,* 3/16/2016) The Middle Ages appeared to offer somewhat more emotional stability for the individual through communal social ties, and obligations of manor life. However, this is open to question, given the level of poverty and abandonment in the lives of the common people.

In the course of history, individual desires had become proscribed; social custom, and laws both judged and adjudicated sexual behavior. Foucault (1978) indicates that despite all the various customs that dominate our lives, sex is the "explanation for everything" (p.78), and "It will be granted no doubt that relations of sex give rise in every society, to a deployment of allure: a system of marriage, of fixation and development of kinship ties, of transmission of names and possessions." (p. 106).

The Middle Ages, as Philippe Ariès (1960) relates, witnessed the ascendancy of the Church, with its increased railing against promiscuity and assertion of the value of virginity. Still, contradictory forms of sexual behavior occurred, almost in parallel process, and pointed to the various and opposing forces operative simultaneously in society. The Church, though preaching virtuous and abstinent behavior from the early inception of Catholicism, especially for religious leaders, priests and monks, witnessed fornication, and fathering of children by Bishops and Popes, throughout early, middle, and late medieval times. The Catholic Church finally forbade marriage for its clergy in the twelfth century at the Second Lateran Council in 1139, and reaffirmed celibacy in 1563 at the Council of Trent. As the Church gained economic and political power, so too did the secular economic and political forces that were coming to the fore. We witness the rise of individual fiefdoms, feudal lords, and the increased power of kings. Nationalism was on the rise, the birth of a new mercantile class, and the rise and fall of various states and countries all depict the scene. Peasantry was beginning to decline, and the development of guilds and urbanization was becoming the new form of social structure. All attest in various aspects to the changing of times, the rise and fall of one economy supplanted by another, and the many wars. And within this era, both restricted and wanton sexuality seemed to exist side by side. History attests to the ever-persistent increase in laws regulating sex; yet despite laws and edicts, especially those beginning to emanate from the Catholic Church, the cauldron of sexuality defies the constraints imposed upon it.

I will introduce the Troubadours, a romantic and emblematic group of the Middle Ages, at this point in this historical review, for they provide an excellent example of the main currents regarding love and warfare, and their songs and poems provide a window into the dominant mores of the aristocracy, the feudal lords, kings, the Church, all powerful rulers of this society. Courtly love, promiscuous love, conquest of the lady, and fiefdoms to conquer ruled the day. Light is also cast upon the peasant class. The Troubadours (Lindsay, 1973), representing essentially the feudal elite, made both love and war a primary profession, and developed the first instances of what is called "vernacular poetry," (*i.e.* everyday speech). The Troubadour, in his heart and in his mind, called for unfettered love, unlimited boundaries, and suggested what civilization has always struggled to attain, perfect pleasure. And yet there was the recognition that this undiluted pleasure had to be modified in order for societies to maintain order and cohesion.

" I love, but do not know her name.
We've never met; it's all the same.
I've nothing then to praise or blame,

and that's my aim.
No Frenchman or Norman ever came
to explain the game." (Guilheim, 12th century, p.13, in Lind-
    say).

Thus, we hear both love (or sex) and war addressed in the
same stanza.

It's mad on such a love to stray;
She's never made me sad or gay;
For, missing, her, I smile and say:
Here's holiday!
I find a fairer one who'll play a better way. (*ibid*, p.13).

Just as free-floating sexual desire is espoused, so too is the
passion for one ardent love. Guilhem de Poitou, the renown Troubadour of the 12th century whose exploits with numerous ladies
were well-known and infused his poetry, wrote with longing for the
one joy, a perfect lady, "the loveliest heard or seen is she." (quoted
by Lindsay, 1973, p.17) In "Ab la dolcher," he will exclaim "Our
love, I find, is surely now. . . . That morning I remember—how our
conflict ended with a vow." She gives him a ring and he: "Beneath
her cloak my hands will be. . . ." (p. 17) This true love does not
relate to marriage, and the morning after is the consummate expression of sex and love. Other poems by the Troubadours attest
to love for the lady of the manor, the wife of their lord.

Bogin, in her book *The Women Troubadours* (1973), raised
the issue of platonic love as the underlying message, not lust. She
indicated that the licentious behavior ascribed to the Troubadours,
especially random infidelity at Court, posed the danger of impreg-
nation and the Church's ostracism. This appeared too great a risk,
as was the danger from the powerful and jealous lord, if caught.
She further questioned if in reality the praising and elevation of
the lord's wife really represented a very practical undercurrent of
political expedience, in that the Troubadour gained recognition
and power from his lord by praising his wife? Many of the poems
by the Troubadours also shift from the bawdy, and the extolling of
love of women, to the love of God. Wanton love is relinquished—"all

that I used to love I quit. . . . Such is God's will." (Lindsay, 1973). Since we have no statistics, and few personal diaries, we are left to interpret the songs, the poems of the Troubadours as we deem. They certainly indicate a good deal of infidelity and promiscuity.

That there were female Troubadours comes as some surprise, and as Bogin indicates, little scholarship has been awarded to the study of them. She notes that there were about twenty female Troubadours, all from the aristocracy and all married. Their poetry differs from their male counterparts in that there is less idealism and desire for ethereal love, and more reality. The style is similar, but the content reveals plain desire, pain, and distress with love and sex. Isabella decries: Elias Cariel, I want to know the truth about the love we two once had; so tell me, please why you've given it to someone else . . . or

> Elias Cariel, you're a phony
> If I ever saw one,
> like a man who says he's sick
> when he hasn't got the slightest pain.

Is this unrequited love or just a sexual affair?—for Isabella is married, and obviously Elias betrays her; even a fling brings pain.

> Castelloza, distressed laments:
> Handsome friend, as a lover true
> I loved you, for you pleased me
> but now I see I was a fool,
> for I've barely seen you since.

And Anonymous questions her once entranced Knight:

> Friend, I know well enough how skilled
> you are in amorous affairs,
> and I find you rather changed
> from the chivalrous knight you used
> to be. I might as well be clear,

for your mind seems quite distracted:
do you still find me attractive? (Bogin, 1973)

The male Troubadours pronounce love and even pain at denial of their quest, and in a lofty voice produce more song; while the women Troubadours suffer the "slings and arrows" of betrayal and neglect from real men. The women poets give sufficient evidence that the sexual behavior was more than platonic, and involved sexual intercourse. This is contrary to Bogin's belief that infidelity and licentious sexuality was more in the word than in the act.

Chaucer's Canterbury Tales

Chaucer, whose work spans the latter part of the fourteenth century, provides us with a cast of characters from the bawdy to the religious. We see evidence of the dual forces of the Middle Ages, the secular and the religious, each providing a different view on sexuality. His *Canterbury Tales*, similar in some form to the poetry of the Troubadours, provides a picture of love, warfare, male and female relations, attitudes about children, and the role of the Church in everyday lives. John Miles Foley, in his introduction to Chaucer, recounts the various dimensions of the *Tales*: A Knight will spin a "lofty narrative of romance and cosmology . . . the "lowly Miller will answer with a bawdy story of love . . . while the Reeve will answer with a story of a 'doubly cuckolded miller, ' and another will "chart a middle road of medieval institutions of courtly love and the Christian Church." Chaucer will also provide a view of both the lives and thinking of the aristocracy, and those of the peasants; moral rectitude and hypocrisy, sexual purity, and wanton sex: this was the rule of the day.

In the "Knight's Tale," we are told the story in rhyme of two knights, Arcite and Palamon, Thebans, fighting over the love of Emily, married to Theseus, governor of Athens, who has locked both in prison as captured enemies during a battle. This tale reverts to the idealization of women, for both are in love with an abstract, idealized woman whom they simply observe from the gates of a prison window. As "lovely" Emily alone strolls in the garden, suddenly observed by Palamon : "Is she a woman ? Or goddess? From just what "I have seen, in that narrow window, I believe it is Venus."

And Arcite is also enchanted:

The shining beauty of her, walking this earth,
So overwhelms my heart and being, that unless
She graces me with her lovely glance, and blesses
Me with her heart, so I may walk beside her,
I am as good as dead. It has been decided. (pp. 32, 255)

What should we make of this quality of romanticism, deep love of the unknown, simply seen with one's eyes at a distance? What is the nature of this aspect of sexuality? Can this romanticized love be civilization's way of defending against the plain, lewd, sexuality inherent in human nature that can be aroused by sight: total strangers capable of bringing forth the power of the sexual instinct?

As civilization advanced and the population increased, more and more control over individual behavior was exercised. Without controls, it is possible to envision chaos, sex at every street corner! The wanton love and sexual delights that Chaucer's tales present represent reality but also more fantasy, for he well understood human emotions and desires. Strange as it may seem, writing is culture's way of adding controls to unbridled sexuality; to observe, to feel, to talk, but not to act.

And so the "Miller's Tale," following the edifying story of the gallant Knights, deepens our understanding of sex and love in the Middle Ages, a literary means of both sublimating our instincts, and also reflecting on the current mores.

"The Miller drunk from all the ale he'd downed, . . .
Not a man to doff his cap to the worthy"(p. 85, lines 10–15)

Then he begins his tale about a carpenter and his wife, and a cleric, who "puts a cuckoo cap on the fool." The carpenter's wife had an affair with the young scholar who rented a room in his home. Chaucer's tale defies the rules of religious morality, since the young married wife of eighteen, who attended church regularly, eagerly falls into bed with her lover. Further, a young cleric in the Church tries to seduce her. Chaucer in this witty tale warns against the old who are desirous of the young. "He'd never read Cato's book of maxims, which say that every Man should choose a wife like himself: age and youth will often fight like rats in a cage." Here he gives recognition to what I have indicated as the genetic role that procreation plays in relationships, the older men pursuing youth and beauty, to beget as many offspring as possible. And yet, Chaucer in "The Wife of Bath's Prologue," will also show that procreation need not rule us. There is a gentle protest against the sole purpose of sex for procreation—"God gave his creatures these tools for urine excretion, And also for making new lives in God's creation." Yet "No one must be obliged to populate." (p.162)

That infidelity breaks the bounds of moral teaching, a recognition that Chaucer gives to the range of sexual desire, permeates the *Tales*. Thus, he speaks from the mouth of his character the Wife of Bath:

"For sure, virginity is a great perfection. . . . But gentlemen , excuse me, I couldn't endure it. At whatever age I am, I want to bestow/The flower of my body in the acts and fruits of love." And when her fourth husband died, "Before the month was over, this jolly cleric, Jankyn, who had been my lover, Became my husband, with great solemnity." (pp.161–162)

The Church, marriage, cuckolded men, raunchy women, and docile women and men betrayed and betraying, all have a say in *The Canterbury Tales*. Literature is a great purveyor of the emotions, customs, and behavior of a culture.

Family Structure through the 11th to the 15th Centuries

The writings of the Troubadours and Chaucer create a scenic mood in which to view these centuries, for though much is known of the reality of wars, Church structure and the economics of the society, little is really known of the psychology of individuals regarding their inner feelings about love, betrayal, marriage and children. Songs and stories provide some insight into the inner lives of people and the major concerns of the society, yet they are still stories and not absolute fact.

The history of family life presents us with what seems to be contradictions regarding the attitude toward children. This was a time when childhood was short-lived; familial and filial relationships seemed somewhat distant. Many historians indicated that families during the Middle Ages did not appear to have close ties between married couples, or between children and parents. The rule, according to Ariès (1960) in *Centuries of Childhood,* was to send children away around the age of seven to ten to be apprenticed, to learn how to work, to learn manners, and social customs from another family, or simply to earn a living. The upper-class children who were sent away tended to return to their original home when they were grown, perhaps ten years later. Yet various trends appear in opposition to each other. Often what occurred were various lines of development that proved in later periods to have one or the other become prominent. Some historians, contrary to the usual mode of viewing the parental attitude towards the child as distant, present a picture of a more loving and close relationship. In spite of the accepted practice of sending the child off to be apprenticed to work, or in the care of another family, a large number of families, especially in the upper classes, kept their children at home. The sons, mainly the eldest, and particularly daughters, remained with their natural families. Shulamith Shahar indicates that family life was much more centered on children than has been recognized; thus, within the norm there are various modes of practice.

Life in the early and middle part of the Middle Ages did not appear to be centered on a nuclear family as we now know it; rather, the family was "linear," pretty inclusive: aunts, uncles, cousins, even strangers, paid help, and the apprenticed children all formed part of the familiar structure.

Life tended to be focused outside the home: on the streets, so to speak: the plazas, the fairs, wherever people strolled or did business. This is where social interchange occurred and where relationships were made. The houses also, particularly for the middle and upper classes, were places where people gathered, in an informal mode of visiting and living. Generally the visitors were of the same social class. Yet there was also, a fluid interchange of citizens, a mixture of masters, servants and workers, that became more stratified in later centuries. Rooms were not specified for particular activities; bedrooms could become dining rooms or sitting rooms. The beds were portable, closed up, moved to different rooms or curtained off. Perhaps what is most fascinating was the sleeping arrangements and the lack of privacy. Many people slept in the same room, servants and masters, children and adults, sometimes four beds to a room, women with women, and men with men. In such conditions, the sexual behavior would probably startle our sensibilities, for children of a very young age were constantly exposed to the sexual activities of the adults. Sexuality and lurid talk appeared to have been less secretive than in later centuries. Since marriage at ages 12 to 14 were common, and seven-year olds were already working alongside adults, childhood was not viewed as a special time of innocence, nor was it particularly revered.

Did these patterns of sexual behavior and family fluidity exist at the same time, or on equal footing with the more stringent rules regarding sexual relations and the role of marriage and monogamy? Ideas concerning chastity, and the belief that sexuality existed primarily for procreation purposes, were easily contradicted by the general behavior of the society. It is difficult to get a consistent chronological order of time sequence as to when sexuality succumbed to the rigors of the Church's edicts. There were marked differences in attitude and actions between the upper classes and the working classes, the peasants and the tradespeople for whom the luxury of large homes, many rooms, and wealth to feed many mouths did not exist. Historical data tends to detail the lives of the wealthy, so that a more detailed picture of the peasant and the tradesperson is more difficult to secure. Stark indicates (1985) that the peasant homes consisted of one large room; therefore, the total family, plus help and visitors, all slept huddled together on the floor. Sexual activity between the adults could not be hidden. The poor household generally consisted of 5–6 people, while the wealthy homes generally comprised 10 or more persons.

Women were prolific in childbearing, but the mortality rate was high. One in three infants died before their first year, and one-third generally died on reaching adulthood. Good mothering was what was considered an invention of modernization, since life was so precarious, and marriage and sexual fidelity, despite the laws of the Church, were still loosely followed.

In this feudal, agrarian economy revolving around lords and serfs, marriage, especially for the upper classes and the aristocracy, was an important means of controlling property and continuity of rule. Love and romance, though beginning to influence individual relationships, entered little into these unions. The marriage contract was an important legal document, and marriages were essentially economic and political unions of families. Children as young as seven were often contracted in marriage in order to protect the power and longevity of the family line. Children born out of wedlock among the upper classes were often raised in the father's court or given to other families of the aristocracy. Marriage among the peasant class was represented by simple familial agreement or individual verbal consent. It would appear from the easy entrance into marriage and the ease of divorce, that emotional ties were not very strong, and sexual behavior had minimum constraint. Since deeding inheritance to children played a very minor role, children born out of wedlock did not stain the mother. Children from the peasant class easily became farm workers for the feudal lords or worked as servants at the manor house as young as seven. Sexual relations between the lords and servants were rather the rule than not.

Divorce, as well as trial marriage, known as "Handfasting," was extremely common during the Middle Ages; so was cuckolding by the woman, and infidelity by the man. Thus, side by side with the developing monogamous family, the rise of Church laws regarding marriage rites, and sexual morality, we witness divorce, the ease of prenuptial sexual relations, and adultery (Yalom, 2001).

As feudalism began to decline with the rise of the merchant class and a rising bourgeoisie in the cities, stable marriages increased as they reflected the needs of this new developing economy. Farm communities, the village, and the extended family declined, and thus their customs and their social organization played a lesser role in the new developing urban society. A smaller, more insulated family began to develop that better met the needs of this new economy. Though the ideas concerning marriage still reflected the need to perpetuate the family line and the control of property, the notion of love in a marriage began to permeate the culture. (Yalom, 2001) Further, private marriages that were simply decreed by the couple or family contracts declined as the role of the Church took on the force of law. By the 15th century, the Church began to officiate at wedding ceremonies. Previously, the priest simply blessed the couple outside at the church door: a ceremonial act, not a binding role. Even this was not a necessary requisite for marriage; a sexual relationship and/or a mutual agreement solidified the marriage. During the later Middle Ages, private agreements declined, and the Church became the official organ to legitimize marriage. Gay marriages and male bonding ceremonies were quite common within the church until the thirteenth century.

The role of women during this period also went through an evolutionary cycle. The early development of civilization witnessed women in a fairly equal role with males. As societies became more organized and structured, the power of women declined, and they became increasingly subservient both in law and social custom to males (Fisher, 1992). The peasant women enjoyed even more freedom and control than those of the aristocracy, since property and inheritance were not an important consideration. This, too, began to change with the new order of economic organization, and the role of the church's becoming more influential. Women were viewed as the weaker sex, requiring care and protection from the male.

Barbara Tuchman (1978) noted that by the fourteenth century, as the Church became more powerful, its edicts against sex, adultery, and prostitution became more vociferous. Canon law handed out rather cruel punishment for adultery, and hangings, pillory, and life imprisonment often resulted. While countries varied in the zeal and degree of litigation against infidelity, promiscuity, sodomy, and fornication, the power of secular laws also exerted more power and rule regarding sexual behavior. Yet, the "crimes" of sex continued despite the punishments! The Middle Ages were rampant with sexual promiscuity.

The Late Middle Ages and the Renaissance Period

The fifteenth and the sixteenth centuries represented a refinement and essentially a continuation of changes from the fourteenth century in regard to family life and sexual behavior, and can be further viewed as a transition into a new mode of economic life. The latter part of the fifteenth, and sixteenth, centuries referred to as the Renaissance are exemplary for their art, wars, piety, fornication, and the power of kings and the Church.

From the middle of the seventeenth century, changes in family structure and relationships between parents and children that were developing during the Middle Ages began to accelerate. Hierarchical class structure took on additional elements. Where previously the system consisted principally of nobles, gentry and the peasants (or yeomen), additional categories arose, such as merchants and tradesmen, professionals, and a new rising middle class. Increasingly, children remained at home, schooled by tutors, or were sent to boarding schools where there was constant interaction with the biological parent. The rise of public schools in this period for the poorer population was a momentous occurrence. The open-house custom dwindled; visiting as casual dropping in now required a more planned entrance. Defined visiting hours became the custom, and strangers no longer freely occupied beds in the house. The focus shifted from the outside to the inside. Concern with children became important, and the relationship between husband and wife witnessed a shift from simple compatibility to a closer, more intimate affair. Marriages that had been solely devised for property, family alliances, or convenience now began to take on an emotional tone of love.

Psychology, the internal processes of the mind, now entered into the marriage arrangement and began to influence sexual behavior. Emotions that in previous cultures had been defined by different standards now demanded a new set of behaviors from spouses. Not only did the economy, the means of working in a mercantile society based on a small cottage industry with increased commerce, change the nature of family relationships, but a new mindset developed that viewed monogamy and adultery with a different set of expectations. The psychologist and the sociologist may well ask: how do economic and political forces change basic biological instincts and therefore, influence not only actual behavior but also mental ideas? In essence, how did the changing economic and political structures result in changing sexual behavior, particularly attitudes about monogamy and infidelity? We know that divorce became harder to attain, particularly for the middle and peasant classes, due to the great expense that it incurred. Parliament and the ecclesiastic courts had become the arbiters of divorce, and generally divorce was granted mainly for adultery. Since laws against adultery were so cruel and life-threatening, we could assume that fidelity became more the norm. Yet, since there were so many abandoned women and children, particularly in England, who ended up in the poorhouse, we must presume that infidelity played a large part in these desertions due to the fear of punishment. The answer to our question above lies in that intricate balance between biology and environment. Quantity and quality will eventuate in the ultimate outcome of the various forces facing individuals and society. (Freud, 1927, [1930])

Further, books such as *The School of Venus* or *Ladies' Delight* (Millott 2017) give some indication that sex, far from suffering total repression and control by law and religion, continued to play an active role in these centuries. A particular poem, "The Young Damsel's Lamentation," expressing the wish to be deflowered, to be "punched," is an indication of the flourishing sexuality.

"Was it not a pleasure to every handsome maid,
 When first they heard the tidings of the new Punching trade;
     and
Of course a truth it was we know,
They with cheerful hearts did go.

So, despite the pious statements from the Church and secular or royal law, it is not possible to leave the seventeenth century without acknowledging the amount of promiscuity, adultery and infidelities that were dominant in the culture.

Chapter Six
The Victorian Era—
England and The United States

The Victorian Era exemplified the power of the Church by its ability to solidify control over marriage and sexual behavior. This could not have happened if the economic realities of a bourgeois and industrialized society were not the prime movers of the cultural ethic. An independent nuclear family that relied upon husband and wife, especially the male, for economic support, appeared to fit the needs of an urban industrial society. The nature of work, the long hours, the dedication to the factory or shop that characterized the industrial society brought with this a regulated work ethos, and therefore, a more regimented social structure. Anna Walker (1866) a poet, extols work as a value unto itself:

> Work, for the night is coming:
> Work, through the sunny noon;
> Fill brightest hours with labour,
> Rest comes sure and soon.
> Give every flying minute
> Something to keep in store:
> Work, for night is coming,
> When man works no more. (Mitchell's *Daily Life in Victorian England*, p. 261)

The requirements to attend work daily and at specified hours, and to travel to places at specific times, required a cohesive family structure that could attend to and support these prescribed behaviors. Therefore, a stable marriage with adequate care for children and proper schooling best met the needs of this new economy. Adultery, licentious sexuality, interfered with a stable home life; and thus the dictates of the Church regarding promiscuous sexual behavior attained greater support from all classes. Further, secular law reinforced the Church's edicts, and issued its own harsh punishments regarding what was considered immoral sexual behavior. With urbanization and factory work, the old relationship between the gentry and the villagers rapidly declined. Though poverty had existed among the peasantry, the nature of village and communal life had offered somewhat greater protection against the social hazards of early deaths and abandonment by spouses. The manor lords also offered emotional support and economic protection to those working on their estates as field hands or as domestic workers. Urban life for the new working class was more isolated, and the cohesiveness of the linear family began to disintegrate. Under these conditions, the nuclear family of husband, wife and children became more interdependent. (Flanders, 2003)

Romantic marital relationships that had begun to arise during the late Middle Ages and Renaissance periods became the norm. The economic changes not only affected the nobility and the landed gentry, but also the new working and professional classes. Though political and economic factors continued to influence the attitudes of the upper classes, love was also sought after in their relationships. In this changed social and psychological atmosphere, monogamy and adultery had consequences for the emotional state of the individual. That individual's sexual behavior became increasingly constricted by the demands for conformity, and further by the psychological and emotional needs and desires in this new cultural norm that emphasized love between the spouses (Flanders, 2003)

The Victorian Era, in contrast to the Middle Ages, in which women had a significant amount of independence, and even certain rights to ownership of property, saw an erosion of many of these powers. The husband became viewed as the dominant figure in the home and in society; he was now the lawgiver and provider, limiting women's independence. The philosopher John Ruskin wrote:

"The man's power is active, progressive, defensive. He is eminently the doer, the creator, the discoverer, and the defender. His intellect is for speculation and invention; his energy for adventure, for war. . . . But the woman's power is for rule, not for battle, and her intellect is not for invention or creation, but for sweet ordering, arrangement and decision. . . . Her great function is Praise. . . . .By her office and place, she is protected from all danger and temptation. The man . . . guards the woman from all this; within his house, as ruled by her, unless she herself has sought it, need enter no danger, no temptation. . . . This is the true nature of home: it is the place of Peace; the shelter, not only from all injury, but from all terror, doubt, and division. ("Of Queen's Gardens," Mitchell, p.266)

Ruskin's lofty thinking is quite different from the lusty passions and betrayals of the Troubadours, and Chaucer's and Shakespeare's intrigues, female/ male conflicts, and passionate love.. Sex is now a product of domesticity and marriage.

Yet, as Mitchell points out, every "stereotype contains irreconcilable contradiction. Although the (middle-class) woman was legally subordinate, economically dependent, and always obedient to her husband, she was somehow supposed to rule the home. . . . Marriage was seen as woman's natural and expected role: it satisfied her instinctual needs, preserved the species . . ." Women were to be kept safely at home, for their compliance, obedience and innocence made them easy victims in the "competitive public world." The pure woman preserved the higher moral values, "guarded her husband's conscience," and "regenerated society through her daily display of Christianity in action." If she succeeded in making a peaceful, loving home, her sons and husbands would not leave for an evening of entertainment or pleasure elsewhere. Obviously, this must allude to the "club" or house of prostitution. On the one hand, women were to be powerful in the home, keep order, rule, yet be subservient. This certainly contained an inherent contradiction for women's psyche. It is difficult to be a ruler and subservient at the same time. Marriage had become central for the ideal image of womanhood, it was the defining image for her; it defined her role, her rank, duties and social status.

A poem by Alfred, Lord Tennyson, "The Princess" (1847), provides a clue to what even men of great intellect and creativity regarded as women's role, and how they conceived of their emotional and sexual needs.

Man for the field and woman for the hearth;
Man for the sword, and for the needle she;
Man with the head, and woman with the heart;
Man to command, and woman to obey;
All else confusion.

This was a time of double standards. Women were to be pure, to be virgins, to abstain from extramarital affairs, while men, especially upper-class men, were known to have mistresses and illegitimate children. By the 1840s, it became more judicious for men to be quiet about their premarital and extramarital affairs. The Church's teaching regarding morality had finally permeated the entire culture to the degree that sex was seen as something shameful, to be hidden and secretive. Maiden girls were to know nothing of sex, even on their wedding night; it was left to the man to enlighten them. Exciting dances and explicit novels were socially prohibited. Even young adult men were warned against the immorality of premarital sex, masturbation, and visits to prostitutes. One may well question how it was possible to so repress sexuality, which had such free rein in the Middle Ages, to such a quiescent place in the Victorian period? These religious and moral attitudes dominated not only the middle classes but also the upper class and the "respectable working class." The level of concern regarding sexual behavior inside and outside of marriage obviously indicated, as Mitchell comments, a great deal of preoccupation with sexuality and its indulgence.

Hidden behind these moral precepts we find another interesting aspect of Victorian life. It was estimated by historians that about a third of the women who walked down the aisle in England were pregnant, thus providing an interesting contradiction between moral percepts and reality. The statistics of the period indicate that in the United States in 1760 the premarital pregnancy rate 35 percent, declined to ten percent in the 1850s and increased to 25 percent in the late 1860s. Further, diaries and letters of this period reflect a rather erotic atmosphere between husband and wife and also the non-married; Laura Lyman wrote to her husband ". . . I'll drain your coffers dry next Saturday I assure," (Kim Murphy, 2011). Mabel Loomis wrote in her diary after spending a passionate night with her fiancé: "I woke up the next morning very happy though, and feeling not at all condemned." Erotic sex and love were beginning to merge in a more romantic relationship between men and women, despite the moral prohibitions emerging from the ecclesiastic and legal power structures of the society.

Prostitution in the Victorian Era:
Women's Rights and Sexual Behavior

The answer to the question as to how it was possible during the Victorian Era to convince a majority of the culture to so repress nature's sex drive, perhaps lies partially in the human ability to tolerate hypocrisy. A vast underground for sexual pleasure was created, an increase and abundance of houses of prostitution. Women were considered to be largely non-sexual, to have passion primarily for child-rearing and love of their husbands, and were denied the social recognition of their basic sexuality; men continued to take pleasure in houses of prostitution or from the more lowly "street walker."

Prostitution was frowned upon, and prostitutes did not share the same regard as the "moral women"; nevertheless, prostitution was a lucrative business that provided women with a higher level of economic security than that enjoyed by many of middle-class women. They owned property, bought land, houses, and opened businesses. Especially in the "Wild West," that was expanding in territory, houses of prostitution grew exponentially. More men than women settled the West, and, since sexual desires could not be litigated away, prostitution flourished. It is reported that in the early nineteenth century Boston had about two thousand prostitutes, and London was reported to have eighty thousand prostitutes. Gradually the sex trade in America equaled if not surpassed that of Europe. Karen Abbott (2008), in her book *Sin in the Second City*, provided a cast of characters, madams and courtesans, all personages in Chicago during the latter nineteenth century and early twentieth century, which convey the psychological and social dimensions of prostitution. Two sisters, Mina and Ada Everleigh, resourceful and elegant madams, established a high-class brothel for the finest men of the town. Their grand house, furnished in impeccable taste, catered to the politicians, the professionals, and the wealthy. The Everleighs were entrepreneurs who understood the psychological and sexual needs of these men. The "girls" were trained how to behave, how to seduce, to recite poetry, and dress with the elegance of upper-class women. Their brothel was run much like the beginnings of corporate America, a consummate business enterprise. The girls generally came from poverty-stricken homes, or homes that were broken.

That prostitution became a way to earn more money than the harsh conditions of a factory does not really explain why women would enter into a trade so degraded in the eyes of the world, and into a brothel system that kept them in, if not total, partial bondage. Further, many sought out men who took their money and to whom they were in emotional bondage. Since no explanation fits all, it is possible to suggest that perhaps a prime and underlying motivation was a curious identification with men's sexuality and at the same time a hatred of men, a very ambivalent attitude. As the prostitute, you subject the man to your ministrations, you are superior, you have the power to please without wanting anything from him; you know his very need as you understand and identify with him, and you can supply or withhold your sexual wares in very subtle ways. Yet, as the prostitute, so powerful with the men subservient to you, fundamentally, in apposition, you, too, are in bondage both to the madam and to the pimp. This is an interesting ambivalent resolution between power and subservience. Abbott, in her analysis of the Everleigh sisters, felt that despite their keen understanding of men and the culture of prostitution, they basically hated men.

In America, the Puritans would find in Victorian morality an emblem of their faith (Flanders, 2003); and that America simultaneously could be a land where prostitution flourished so successfully raises some interesting areas for perusal. A theory was espoused for men in the 1870s as the "doctrine of necessity." Officials and medical authorities in New York City proclaimed "prostitution helped men diffuse tension without offending the sexual mores of their wives, who were restricted under the ideals of Victorian sexuality." (Jackson, 2004, p.3). Since prostitutes were considered corrupt by nature, they required neither the concern of society nor protection against sexual abuse or rape. A statement such as this gives license not only to prostitution, but also to infidelity, despite the high regard for monogamous marriages.

Parallel to the rise of the hidden and secret "vice of prostitution" was the rise of the Women's Movement that fought for equal rights between men and women, and played a role in bringing to the fore issues of sexuality. Some historians have noted that public discourse about sex came into prominence during the nineteenth century. A scientific discourse on sex by physicians arose, though it mainly placed women's sexuality within the mores and ideas of the Victorian image of the sweet, unpassionate woman whose purpose was to serve her husband. The concept of nymphomania was coined to describe a woman desirous of frequent sex, and of course was disparaging towards women. Yet a recently found research study done between1892 and 1920 by Dr. Clelia Duel Mosher revealed that married Victorian women talked more about sex and the pleasures of making love than was acknowledged; this would indicate that the taboos about sexual enjoyment by women and their interest in sex did not present an accurate reflection of the realities of Victorian life. Did Victorian women engage in extramarital relations or premarital sex? Contraception methods were developing rapidly during this time and therefore, afforded greater sexual freedom for women. Further, literature reveals to us what was pertinent in the culture. Hawthorne's (1850) *Scarlet Letter*, the story of Hester Prynne, though set in the seventeenth century, relates the story of a single woman, who is pregnant; the writings of Hardy (1891), such as *Tess of the d'Urbervilles*, Flaubert's (1821) *Madame Bovary*, and Tolstoy's (1877) *Anna Karenina*, attest to sex outside of marriage and premarital sex. Still, taboos regarding sexuality influenced the major thinking and overt behavior of nineteenth-century Victorian society.

To return to the place of prostitution not only in the Victorian period, but also throughout history, we may ask why married men seek other women to engage in sexual activities? Religious prohibitions against frequent sex by married couples, and various erotic possibilities could induce a rebellious response, and therefore, partially explain the fascination with prostitution. We indicated earlier that sex is driven by the biological need to procreate, and that man is driven to implant his seed with frequency. Does this help explain the drive for different sexual objects to woo and to seduce, even though the prostitute is not considered a source for procreation? Yet the drive to discharge one's seed continues to propel men sexually. Ryan and Jetha (2014) concluded in their book on sexuality that men more than women are driven by their evolutionary biology to seek out a variety of sexual objects, despite the fact that they may love their monogamous partners. The sexual drive in men, as evidenced by the amount of testosterone in their bodies, largely accounts for their behavior. How else to explain the inability to maintain the ties of monogamy by so large a number of the male population? Ryan and Jetha indicated that our puritanical codes on sex, in essence by proclaiming false values on sexual behavior, inadvertently contribute to the high rate of divorce. Perhaps we may add to the list of biological incentives, the role of the "selfish gene" first explicated by Dawkins (2006) that ensures survival of the individual's body, taking precedence over reproduction. This selfish gene is a genetic holdover from the very first origins of mankind, and thus sexual satisfaction in various forms and with various mates drives human sexual behavior.

Yet there are additional explanations, such as characteristics of a psychological wish for power, an aspect of our aggressive nature that impels men to seek and conquer, and thus conquering women can also satisfy this aggressive need. Further, we can also seek possible answers in the nature of family life, the relationship of the child to both mother and father, and the long years of dependency. In these relationships, we are bound to encounter sexual feelings. Societies from earliest times have erected laws against incest, and despite the breaking of incest taboos by many, we continue to value this taboo as sacred, an important moral issue for the good of society. The family, as a small nuclear unit of man and woman that developed from the seventeenth century on, probably was an even greater stimulus for old childhood sexual attractions to both parents. It is no accident that wife is often called Mother by the husband rather than by name. The distant man or woman, or the prostitute, can free one of these memories, even though they may exist in the deepest recesses of the unconscious. Prostitution permits a guilt-free sexual encounter, a distance from the incest remnants, and a decidedly pleasurable experience, free from the stresses of a solid loving marriage or relationship. Since incestuous wishes also apply to women, we need to consider other factors that deflect her sexuality. Perhaps her role in childbearing and in nurturing the child is able to sublimate her sexual drives, and thus accounts for her lower levels of infidelity, and not as frequently seeking out the male prostitute.

Alexa Albert, in her book *Brothel,* indicated that both single and married men were frequent visitors to Mustang Ranch, a rather classy brothel in Nevada that catered to the rich and famous, including illustrious politicians. Understanding the curious contradictory behavior that both espoused the religious morality against prostitution and the engagement in this illicit behavior asks that we re-examine our concept of hypocrisy. Though I have cited the religious and legal objections to prostitution and adultery as hypocritical, I would like to suggest another, more complicated, concept that may provide additional insight into the phenomena. Hypocrisy suggests a conscious awareness of an act or of conflicting ideas. The decision to advocate one idea openly while criticizing the other, though secretly acting on it, is due to a particular self-interest, or an economic or political gain. The second concept refers to another psychological mechanism, referred to as isolation. (Eissler, 1958) Both ideas, the wish for prostitution or wanton sex, and feelings that they are immoral and need to be curtailed, exist side-by-side. Since the person cannot resolve both desires in a more conscious and rational manner, they are separated and isolated from each other in such a way that the mind negates the fact that they offer conflicting messages to the conscious mind. There is a mental failure to register their inherent opposition; so that one may fight against "immoral sexual" behavior and at the same time engage in the very activities that one opposes, a very neat psychological trick.

Since the nature of sexuality has such a wide range of interesting components, we also need to understand the whips and lashes in the sex act, the enjoyment of inflicting pain, and the pleasure thus received. Fists inserted into the anus causing fissures and bleeding, being tied to a post, physically hit, raped—these acts were a component of sexuality in the Victorian Era. The assumed first pornography book, *The Life and Adventures of Fanny Hill* by John Cleland, written in the eighteenth century, finds numerous echoes in the pornographic books of the Victorian Era. Homosexuality, bisexuality, crossdressing, group sex, bawdy nuns and salacious priests—all are subjects for pornographic literature. The Marquis De Sade, in his *One Hundred Days of Sodom,* written in the latter part of the Victorian Era, brings together a range of sexual fantasies that involve rape, incest, tearing of flesh, beatings, and finally murder of victims as young as thirteen. The connection between sex and murder in De Sade brings into relief the very close interaction between the sexual drive and the aggressive drive. It enables us to comprehend the intertwining relationship between murder and rape, the underlying pleasure that the perpetrators of these crimes experience. *Venus in Furs*, written by Leopold von Sacher-Masoch in 1870, is a tale of masochism and homosexuality, and the semi-autobiographical historical fiction *Romancing The Countess*, by Ashley March (2011), and *The Nunnery Tales*, Anonymous, all tell lurid stories of sadism, masochism, sexual behavior by nuns and priests, flagellations and spankings, homosexual activity, and incest. Nothing is left to the imagination, and these stories were common in this most sexually conservative era, The Victorian Era. While Ryan and Jetha indicate that repression and denial of sexuality frequently lead to more aggressive behaviors, it is also apparent that in sadomasochism there is a blending of the two biological drives in such a manner as to produce a sexually gratifying experience. Perhaps this can also explain the power of rape. a fusion of the sexual and aggressive drives in such a way that violence produces sexual pleasure.

As we depart the Victorian Era for the next century, we may well ponder how it was that so much hypocrisy around sex and social repression could have dominated a culture as sophisticated as this period. The literature, the economic advancements, the scientific discoveries, and social changes attest to an enlightened civilization, and yet, the sexual doctrines signal a society of dark ages.

Chapter Seven
The Twentieth and Twenty-First Centuries: The United States

The latter part of the twentieth century and the beginning of the twenty-first bear little resemblance to prior centuries; economic environment, bodily appearance, dress, and physical landscape all attest to a vastly different scene. Cities abound with colossal structures, beyond the imagination of our ancestors. Hordes of people dominate the earth, and mass transportation can take us on endless journeys. Airplanes, like birds, circle the world; there are television, apps, and smart phones. We have the capacity to communicate worldwide in an instant with total strangers. The Internet, computer, and television have all created a global world of social intercourse. Is it possible to consider that these technological changes have modified our genetic structure (Lamarck) in the way we think and act and desire, or are we unchanged in our genes? Do sexual desires, reproductive aims, and aggression, continue to define us, as always, like the human of ancient times? Further, the brilliance of technology is so extensive that modern man can clone animals, and perhaps, someday humans will be cloned. Our technology has so profoundly changed the nature of human interaction that our mentality appears vastly different from past generations.

Regardless of these major social changes, I suspect that we remain fairly consistent to our past modes of sexual desire. Basic biological and emotional needs of men and women persist, despite the fact that they have undergone significant psychological diversity in their outward expression, as a result of the changed economic, technological, and social conditions. (Boteach, 2008). We may also ask whether our aggressive behaviors have also been modified as a result of these great technological developments. Unfortunately, wars continue to erupt with frequency, rape, castration, and brutal killings remain, and we have become even more skillful in developing the engines of global destruction. We have advanced in our techniques to destroy, and also in ways to engage in sex.

As we pursue our inquiries about monogamy, adultery and sexual patterns in this modern era, what do we observe? We have advanced from the secretive and repressive conventionality of the

Victorian Era, and claim that sex reaches beyond the biological drive to just procreate. We have become more sophisticated in our sexual expressions and capacity to satisfy both men and women. The culture has become "sexually savvy," and what was once a private encounter in the bedroom is now available for all to see. Sexuality has become a commercial product. The number of self-help books, instructions in "how to do," how to seduce and allure the other, and how to improve marital sexual relations, appear everywhere. Sex therapists have become the norm, and movies and television are not shy about showing nudity, sexual seduction, and simulated sexual intercourse. The commercialization of sex appears to rule the twenty-first century, and indicates a high degree of preoccupation with sex, *(The Sex Myth*, Hills, 2015). Margaret Mead, the prominent anthropologist, in her study *Male and Female: a Study of Sexes in a Changing World* (revised since its first publication in 1949) was prescient in understanding the effects of commercialized sex on individual behavior and self-assessment. The self, she indicated, especially for the female, is viewed through the mirror of hairstyle, make up, and stylized beauty that often bears little resemblance to the actual looks and shape of most women and men. Certainly, each culture defines appropriate sexual behavior, from permissiveness, to enlightenment, to tight control, and has its own standards for looks and appearances. The question is how reflective the standards are of real human beings and their behaviors. Ian Smith (2013) in *The Truth About M*en, a bestselling "how to" book, provides instruction for women as to how to arouse a man sexually, how to look, how to attract and keep a man. A survey of 10, 000 men regarding their attitudes toward a woman's body indicated they would dump the woman if she became fat. The stress in Dr. Smith's book on female body care and beauty, reflects a dominant trend in our culture.

What is the meaning of all this emphasis upon sexual behavior; why all this concentration on sex and beautiful bodies? We live in a world where the daily demands of work, taking care of children, the poor, the aged, and struggles to fend off the ravages of wars are ever-pressing. And yet sex appears to dominate our minds and bodies.

Western Civilization from the twentieth century into the twenty-first has been called a time of "sexual revolution." We refer to this as a revolution despite the facts that sex during the Middle Ages, particularly the early half was marked by perhaps as great a degree of sexual freedom, divorce, adultery, and easy sexual encounters. We further assume, a rather valid assumption, that prehistoric man had infinite sex. That the twentieth century is regarded as a time of revolution is a likely reaction to the repressive and hypocritical mores and constraints of the nineteenth century. In many ways, we have neglected the knowledge of history, and seem to have to relearn it in every generation. Yet there appears to be something different in our current sexual behaviors from those of the past libertine societies. Somehow the behavior of sex in past societies was governed by structured patterns of family life that now seem to be discarded. As Mead (1949) pointed out, the learning from past generations, the memory of accepted behaviors has been lost, and this generation must educate itself, must establish new norms.

Jack Meyers (2012), in *Hooked Up*, informs us that the new norm is sex without a relationship, and it appears that many college students are wary of strong feelings for another. A Stanford University study of more than 17 thousand students revealed that 72 percent had experienced at least one hookup by their senior year. Men had on average 9.7 hookups while women averaged 7.1 hookups. These figures do not seem to indicate an excessive amount of sexual activity, unless "hookups" were studied in isolation from other types of sexual relationships. Perhaps, as Rachel Hills (2015) has indicated in her book *The Sex Myth*, the proclamations regarding profuse sexual behavior among the youth is more of a myth than a reality. Though the current media scene is ablast with sex, the statistics vary. One study by "Alice" (Internet, 2016) indicated that "Hooking Up" occurred in 53% to 76% of the student body. "College Sex: The Introduction" by Lauren Kern and Noreen Malone (2015) in *The Sex Myth* pointed out that "College sex was both a playland and a minefield." 25 percent of college women reported rape. *New York Magazine* reported that forty percent of students were virgins, indicating that sixty percent were non-virgins. Sexual freedom appeared as much a burden as a gift. In a 20-year study of college students by Dr. Sandra Caron, released in 2012, 43 percent of girls were virgins. This translates into 57 percent of girls' having had sexual intercourse by the time they graduated. Certainly sexual intercourse with a variety of partners is the predominant mode of sexual activity prior to marriage. Essentially, what are the implications for marital relationships and for society?

The social ideology regarding the sexual body, especially for women, is an important component in establishing the sense of self, and self-worth. (Kimmel, 2008). Unfortunately in this current atmosphere self-concepts regarding one's integrity as a woman or man are unduly distorted by the ideology of sex and body beauty. The claims of sexual intercourse as a *must* that infuse the thoughts of high school and college students is still a reality, whether acted upon or not. Sex as a dominant force in social relationships has distorted the perceptions of self for so many young women and men. They begin to doubt their worth as individuals if in any way they do not feel sexually desirable to the other sex. Hills poses an interesting psychological dilemma for the youth of today, in that the media is so powerful that countering its sexualized images appears almost insurmountable.

Further, Meyers indicates that quick sex as a desired goal raises more questions regarding this behavior since in essence it belies what is emotionally desired in the human interaction, a permanent or a meaningful emotional tie to another. We witness contradictory forces, and since the media is so powerful, it becomes more difficult to challenge its message, and to deny the realities of its precepts. This remains a powerful factor, despite the realities of opposing internal awareness and quests for a more truthful self-validation (Kimmel, 2008).

Social Media

The social media are often reflective of real life, and factual evidence can also portray the fantasy life of a culture and its collective unconscious wishes. Yet it is also capable of creating a culture that is antithetical to realistic human needs. Its power, through visual, verbal and auditory methods that send repeated collective messages, tends to become overwhelming for the mind, especially the young mind. Thus, the media has become a social power structure that is capable of arousing and utilizing our basic instinctual drives, our sexuality and our aggression, in ways that are frequently destructive to individual and group needs. The capacity of the media to control and influence an entire society is rather startling. How many of us stop to reflect on this reality?

Movies, which are an invention of the early twentieth century, together with TV that emerged in the 1940s, have the ability to reflect basic elements of our culture but also have the capacity to dominate our aesthetic and moral values. What began as a depiction of human relationships either tragic or humorous has traipsed into voyeurism of the naked body and sexual acts. In the past, sex, romance, and even murder were secondary to the daily struggles of people, their inner psyche, and their interactions with a complex social world. To study the movies and TV in the present era as opposed to much of the past is to be titillated by sex and aggression, and not very concerned with the fundamental complexities of life. Perhaps, representative of the beginning of sadism in movies morph into *Nine and a Half Weeks* (1986) or *Secretary* (2000); or just plain unsaturated sex such as *Risky Business* (1983), *Henry and Jane* (1997), and finally in 2014, *Gone Girl*, a tale of killing and bloody sex scenes. TV movies echo Hollywood in the HBO series *Sex in the City*, Premium cable with *Queer as Folks* (2005), *Entourage* (2004), *Californication* (2007), and *Spartacus* (2010). These movies and TV programs do not represent the minority, the secretive aspects of our culture, but rather are exemplary portraits of what the current culture is becoming. They represent, 24 hours a day, a media culture that permeates our guts and minds. And, if one desires pornographic pleasures, it is no longer necessary to find discreet houses in the red-light district or upper-class venues, when the Internet can supply one with a direct visual turn-on, or means of contacting real live providers of pleasure. The accessibility, even for the young, can be disconcerting. The BSDM site (Bondage and Discipline—Bondage and Submission and Sadism and Masochism), claiming a membership of 1, 444, 086, can be reached at the touch of a finger; and there you may enjoy a multitude of fantasies such as Daddy/ Daughter, role-playing an incestuous relationship. Pornography sales annually reached fifty-seven to one hundred billion dollars. (Klein, 2012) As Foucault indicated, we are experiencing a paradox in the current society that essentially espouses the morality of the Victorian Era and on the surface preaches sexual repression, but in essence has allowed us to purchase all of our sexuality, even the most private of the perversions. Meyers indicated that fifty universities now offer courses on the subject of pornography.

Is it possible that the sexual behaviors of the past, promiscuous, licentious, adulterous, have really morphed in the twenty-first Century into a dialectical sexuality that has no parallel with its ancestors, except perhaps for the most primitive tribes of early existence? Are we on the cusp of a totally new social, sexual and familial organization that has freed the individual from the constraints of hypocritical sexual morality that denied basic biology, and that tended to restrain individual freedom? Or is it possible that we are caught in a great social hoax that claims to bestow choice, freedom of mind and body, and mobility of place and class? In reality we are thrown a bone of pleasure to ease the "slings and arrows of outrageous fortune." Has this onslaught of sexuality in advertising, movies, TV, books, magazines, trains and buses become a visual drug that stimulates, but dulls our senses to the more basic realities of life? Has the commercialization of sex become the "opiate of the people" (Marx)? Another question that arises: what, if any, is the relationship between unfettered sexual behavior and the break-up of marriages, and a troubled society? Perhaps all our questions result in a quandary with the query: are sexual behaviors causative factors or merely the tacit result of other social forces?

Marriage, Divorce, and Family Structure

Marriages in the latter part of the twentieth and twenty-first centuries are occurring later than in the previous century, and the rate of marriage has declined from the 1960s. A Pew Research study (2013, 2014) has indicated that one in five from the age of 25 and older never marry: the percentage is 23% for men and 17% for women, with the total number in the United States 42 million. More adult children from ages 18–31 live at home with parents. We can assume without much doubt that there is a good deal of sexual activity for the unmarried. The research further indicates that 50 percent of the people felt that society was just as well off if people had priorities other than marriage and children, while 46 percent felt that society is better off if marriage and children are a priority. Though statistics vary regarding adultery, the divorce rate is generally appraised at 40–50 percent of marriages. 41 percent of first marriages, 60 percent of second marriages, and 73 percent of third marriages end in divorce. Children of divorced parents are four times more likely to divorce than couples that have never divorced, and interracial couples have a higher divorce rate. (Eli, Frankel, Northwestern University, Education Resource Center). Cherlin (2010) has indicated that cohabiting relationships are higher in the United States than other developed countries, although, marriage is still the most common living arrangement for raising children. The poor and minority children are most likely to grow up in a single-parent family. The Pew research study (2009, 2011) found that the proportion of Americans who are currently married has been diminishing for decades and is lower than it has been at least half a century. The 1950s and 1960s were known as the "Golden Age" for marriage, as it represented a high nuptial rate and a change from what was considered a companionate type of a relationship to a more romantic, loving relationship. (Klinenberg, 2012). The decline is palpable, and by the twenty-first century barely half of U.S. adults are married, and perhaps what is most interesting is that for Millennials, parenthood is valued over marriage. (Tavernise, 2011, National Marriage and Divorce Rate, Trends Center for Disease Control). Does this attitude help us to understand the increase in single-parent families, and in women having children without marriage? One out of three children are fatherless. It has been proven that children in a two-parent family arrangement fare better educationally than children in a one-parent family system. (Waite and Gallagher, 2000)

Race also plays a role in the history of marriage. Prior to the 1960s, Black men and women married in greater proportion to Whites; yet this "Golden Age" for Whites witnessed a decline for Blacks. This is attributed primarily to the increased loss of employment for Black men. The individual's degree of education also plays a role in the marriage and divorce rate. Could the lower marriage rate and higher divorce rate be due to greater economic frustration in this group? Women with a college degree have a lower divorce rate than those with a high-school-or-lower education level. Statistics also show that the better-educated the male, the less he is given to adulterous behavior. (Besharov and West, Census Bureau Population Survey, 1998)

The moral criticism of adultery remains high, despite the fact that there may even be an increase in adulterous behavior. The Kinsey Reports from 1949 and 1953 estimated that approximately 50 percent of men and 26 percent of women had had extramarital affairs. In the twenty-first century the prediction for adultery is higher, and since statistical studies vary, it would be fair to claim that men's rate of infidelity falls in the range of 33 percent to 70 percent, while the range for women is from 19 percent to 60 percent. Given the wide span, most researchers have concluded that many responders have not been truthful. 76 percent of those who have committed adultery stated that there was nothing wrong with this behavior, while ten percent felt that it was morally wrong. According to a Gallup Poll (2013), 91 percent of adults in the United States feel that adultery is morally wrong. We appear to have a disingenuous attitude regarding sexual behavior, since so many persons commit adultery while at the same time condemning it. Further, the power of religious institutions seem to be declining regarding their ability to influence sexual behavior. At the same time, the force of their edicts appears to hold sway, mentally and legally. It comes as a surprise that currently (2016) in 23 states adultery is still considered a criminal offense, notably in Alabama, Illinois, Michigan, Minnesota, and Wisconsin. And a number of states have laws against cohabiting. The fact that in Michigan and Wisconsin, two rather forward-thinking states, adultery is a felony and punishable with imprisonment reflects the continuous social conflict over monogamy, adultery, sexual infidelity, and promiscuity.

Monogamy, Polyamory, and other Multi-Relationships

Monogamy, that is generally understood to lie within the confines of a legal marriage, that is, a sexual relationship with only one legal partner, must now be extended to include partners living together without the confines of legality. Partnerships are increasing, and the legal marital arrangement appears to have increasing competition from other modes of sexual relationships within the boundary of marriage. Polyamory, a mode of sexual relationship with more than one love, is on the rise, and is exiting from a twilight zone to an open consensus between married couples and others. (This does not involve cheating or lying, but rather open sharing and honest discussion among the individuals who know each other. (Sheff, 2014) Swinging among married couples has also become an established pattern. The number of poly couples in the United States can only be estimated, due to the reluctance of people to reveal the true nature of their relationships. Fear of disapproval, loss of jobs, and other retributions make people very wary of disclosing their status. Sheff, in *Psychology Today* (2014) gives an estimate by Kelly Cookson of approximately 1.2 million to 2.4 million poly couples, and if one includes swinging couples, gay male couples, satellite lovers, the number can be as much as 9.8 million couples. This reflects a strong undercurrent and suggests that the pattern of traditional marriage may be undergoing radical and unsuspected changes that challenge the establishd view of marriage as best suited for society's needs.

Polyamory: An Encounter

I did not know what to anticipate when Rick, a colleague, arranged a dinner meeting with two of his polyamorous friends. As sophisticated and open-minded as I believed myself to be, this was an area that I found difficult to understand. I had to dig deep to find sympathy for those that were trying to find a sensible alternative to monogamy and fidelity through polyamory. It is not easy to change one's orientation.

So there we were—facing each other across a table in a delightful Mediterranean style restaurant in upstate New York. Rick was somewhat new to polyamory, and he was the fifth wheel to the quartet of Bill and Lucy, and Keith and Mary (who were not present). The talk initially was a pleasant interlude before we began to discuss polyamory. Bill was a pediatrician, and was involved with a public-health group that cared for disadvantaged children.

His interest in children living in poverty and their health issues was an interesting contrast to Lucy who was very involved with the banking industry. Bill was quite charming and did most of the talking; he shared easily and revealed that polyamory seemed the best solution to his desires for more than one sexual relationship with a woman. He and Lucy had married a year ago but had been living together for about five years prior to marriage. Perhaps they married because he liked the legal commitment, and also wanted to have children with Lucy. He loved children and felt that in a multi-family atmosphere there would be greater care and love, "an abundance of love for all." Yet, since they were not part of a larger group such as a commune, and lived in separate residences, I wondered how the children would fare in society that was still committed to a nuclear family model and monogamy. He felt that as long as the parents were clear as to their lifestyle, the kids would fare well.[1] Bill was clear that in a poly-relationship honesty with the other and oneself was paramount. Rules had to be established and jointly agreed upon. He had had another partner in this present quintet who had "ditched" him, and it took some time for him to get over this love affair. So now there were just Lucy and Mary. While Lucy was involved with Bill, Keith and Rick, it turned out that the quintet was really expansive, for Lucy was having an affair with another woman who was unknown to the group. Bill had agreed to this relationship, but the unknown question was: did all the others in the group consent to this relationship before it began? Further, is permission needed when one member wants to sleep with others, either momentarily, intermittently, or for the longer term, and how many people are permissible? What were the rules of engagement? I later learned that the rules of engagement applied only for the married couples or those cohabitating. One important rule for a committed couple was that no date with another person was made without the knowledge and consent of the other. Times of leaving and coming home were set, and each committed partner knew with whom the other was out. Those,

---

1. Elizabeth Sheff, in her study of children of Polyamorist families, felt that the children by and large fared well, due to the multitude of people surrounding them and the amount of love and care they received. My own judgment is less certain and it is an area that the future of family relationships will ultimately decide upon.

outside the couplet, were free to pursue whom ever they chose.

Is it possible that polyamory is an attempt to bridge the gap between the human passion for sex with many and another human value, monogamy—to fuse these two elements into a more humanistic and socially acceptable mode of functioning? You can have multiple lovers and sex, but under specific conditions and rules that the partners agree upon. Jealousy is a recognized emotion and it is openly dealt with, talked about, and handled with understanding and decency in the relationship. Bill spoke openly about his initial jealousy of Rick, whom he felt had more in common with Lucy. He was also concerned about Lucy's welfare and how Rick would treat her; would he be kind and caring? Eventually, they all became good friends. I would call this an efficient psychological feat of identification. By identifying with Lucy's needs for emotional protection, Bill could also encompass the relationship with Rick, and thus all could become friends, if not lovers. Thus, this sexual relationship turned into a gain for Bill rather than a loss. Further, it is possible that polyamorous groupings provide a wide range of sexual pleasure through the mental mechanism of fantasy. What is not always carried out at the moment, whether heterosexual, or homosexual, masochistic or sadistic, is gratified through the activity of the others. This form of pleasure that is voyeuristic in fantasy is a gain for the "other" rather than a loss. Is this not what poetry, books, plays and songs provide: an ability to experience a myriad of emotions, situations, even sex and aggression, through other characters? They are capable of draining off some of the power of our own intense emotional desires.

But polyamory has not yet evolved into an accepted social institution, a way in which individuals may conform to socially organized modes of behavior, and thus avoid the stigma of infidelity or being outcasts. Just as polygamy, concubinage, and polyandry attempted to solve certain social problems, and nature's drive for sex and power (*i.e.* aggression), and at times succeeded, so it is possible to conceive that polyamory may lead in the future to a socially adaptive organization. I would add to this new construct of sexual behaviors a most important concern: the need to care for children, overseeing their growth and ultimate contribution to the welfare of society.

Feminine Revolution

Some comment on the feminist revolution is necessary, given that the major change in women's social and domestic roles has also impacted sexual relationships between men and women, marriage, and the divorce rate. The fight for women's equality has a long history, starting with the women's suffragette movement in the 1800s and finally with women's achieving the right to vote in the United States in 1920. The 1960s and 1970s witnessed a resurgence of the fight for women's equality. The fight to achieve equal status and pay with men in jobs, education, the military, and—most important—to redress the balance in the marital relationship, took on added militancy. Since World War II, the vision of women working in factories, in the military, and holding public office has become commonplace. Increasingly, women have become doctors and lawyers, college professors, and judges. The poster of "Rosie The Riveter" in WWII changed the image of women as domestic homemakers to one of workers in the great outside world.

Though women worked long before the 1940s in factories, sweat shops, fields, and cottage industries, the mental image of women was one of being in the home, caring for the children, cooking and cleaning. The new image of women, and their desire to be freed from the sole domain of the home, led to a surge in women's rights movements for equal opportunities and equal pay. A psychological shift in their self-image was perhaps the most important change that occurred. The shift from a passive to an active sense of woman in relationship to man led to untold subtle changes in their relationships.

Though, women had been quite active within the home, their tasks and voices were delineated and curtailed. Now their voices were pervasive, and thus a new mode of working out the lines of authority and roles had to be established (Boteach, 2014; Kimmel, 2008). This was especially so in the sexual relationships between the female and the male. Formerly, the man was the aggressor; he was the pursuer, and the initiator of sex; now the woman applied for this role. Each gender could be both active and passive in the sexual act, and, more important, the woman now demanded equal satisfaction in sex. The sexual domain no longer belonged to the man; he too, had to adjust his psyche to permit another, the woman, her authority in the sexual act.

May we assume that there is some correspondence between divorce and the shift in women's roles? Now that more women worked outside the home and earned their own income, they felt freer to end an unhappy marriage. According to an AARP research study (Internet, 7–1–2015) two-thirds of divorces for couples over the age of forty were initiated by women. The number-one reason given for breaking up the marriage was verbal, physical or emotional abuse: that number was 23 percent. Alcohol and drugs represented 18 percent, and marital cheating 17 percent. That women in their late fifties and sixties are now likely to be holding down good jobs has made divorce less threatening. Still, women who are divorced with young children bear the burden of lesser incomes and tend to suffer severe financial difficulties. Yet, despite the fact that women may endure more economic hardship and emotional insecurity by divorcing, they feel emboldened to take this action.

Sexual Attitudes: Girls are Sluts and Boys are Studs

How can we explain that in the twenty-first century, the era of women's rights and liberation, and the proliferation of sexual activity among teenagers, girls are still referred to as "sluts" and boys as "studs"? It is rather astounding that the moral verbiage of the teenager reflects the repressive morality of the Victorian Era. One could have expected that the sexual revolution would have produced a new language for this generation, a language that reflected a new set of moral and social values, a new ideology that destroyed the old stereotype about men and women. What, we may ponder, has denied this group a different emotional and intellectual basis upon which to judge themselves? Dr. Laura Ponton (2000) in *The Sex Lives of Teenagers*, details with poignant pathos the lives of sexually developed girls, and those who are already sexually active. Melissa, a twelve-year old girl, bright and a gifted artist, already bears the title of "slut" because of her interest in sex and boys. She wears tight T-shirts and high-heeled platforms, and calls boys at their homes. For this, she has the moniker of "slut."

Boys who are super-sexual are called "studs," a name intended as a compliment. Dr. Ponton relates that some boys at school yell at Melissa, who has developed breasts, and has a sexual air, "You know how to do it." That such scorn for the female's sexuality is aroused may cause one to question the male's validation of his own sexuality.

Does our society, beneath all the commercialization of sex and emphasis on teenage sexuality, really send a message that sex is dirty and shameful?

Ryan and Jetha (2014) point to societies, (it must be noted that these societies are tribal and culturally isolated from Western Civilization) where teenage sexuality is encouraged and socially managed, and where women who choose and pick men for sex as easily as the male are treated with regard. What is the failing with Western culture, particularly in the United States, wherein women and girls are pronounced sluts for their sexuality? Behind this so-called moral condemnation lies a great deal of hostility and aggression. Angie (Ponton, 2000) sneaks out of the house with her friend to attend a party with all boys. There, she is given a large amount of alcohol by a method called "funneling"—that is, pouring alcohol down one's mouth. When she is intoxicated and passing out, the boys force her into the sexual act of fellatio.

Eleven percent of female victims of rape are between the ages of 12 to 15, and 25 percent of rape victims are between the ages of 16 and 19. Male youths under 20 are responsible for 18 percent of single rapes and 30 percent of multiple rapes. Sixteen percent of men were sexually abused in childhood, and another study revealed that nine percent of men have been raped (Brookover, 1989; Stolorow & Brandchaft, 1987). This violence clouds the pristine flower of sexuality, and makes us ponder whether Ryan's and Jetha's thoughts that unfettered sex can really reduce violence and aggression are legitimate.

Orenstein (2016) in *Girls & Sex*, similarly gives an unpleasant account of male-female relationships. In the relationships between the sexes, "fully half the girls had experiences something along a spectrum of coercion to rape." (p. 5). Much, she opines, has changed in the public domain, so why not more in the private domain? Let us recall that one of the primary causes for divorce, that is, why women divorce men, is physical and mental cruelty. Boys create Instagrams to alert the school campus as to who are "THOTs," an acronym for "That Ho' Over There," in order to taunt girls who are considered sluts. The Internet has become a vehicle in which both male and female belittle each other, cast sexual slurs, and humiliate. Orenstein has taken issue with the underlying assumptions of the schools, and the general public's attitude about the manner in which girls dress. The overriding opinion is that girls are responsible for the nasty epithets, and rape, because of their provocative dress, the tank tops, the short-shorts, exposed belly buttons, *etc.* She criticizes the blamers and finger-pointers at the girls. And yet she raises some very pertinent issues as to the meaning of the female dress and its high degree of sensuous display. Unfortunately, she indicates, the girls are not experiencing themselves as a subject but are objectifying them-selves, selling themselves as a product to be bought and acquired. How popular are they, how many boys like them, are they pretty enough? She pointed to an interesting study of female graduates at Boston College (2013). Upon graduation, the females have a lower sense of self-esteem than when they entered, and in contrast, the boys have a higher regard for themselves. The focus for females, unfortunately, has assumed an almost obsessive quality regarding their looks and bodies, an objectification that precludes a focus upon their inner self as valuable human beings.

The question that needs to be raised is why the explicitly sexual dress that accentuates all aspects of the female body, at times to partial nudity, has become the dress of choice? This mode of dress is not an aspect of pretty style or pleasing garments, but rather an accentuation of the body. Why has the body so triumphed over the mind and emotions as to leave the female in such an emotional quandary; am I beautiful, am I desired, do I turn them on? This concern with body, with sex, is vastly different from the past, when, as Jane Jacobs Brumberg (in the late 1990s) pointed out in *The Body Project*, women before WWI focused on helping others, becoming better read, and cultivating empathy. "One hundred years later," she writes, "I will lose weight, get new lenses, [have] already got a new haircut, good makeup, new clothes and accessories"—these were the new preoccupations (p.17).

Shall we place blame for this shift, from internal values to an emphasis on more superficial concerns and interests that are guiding current society, on culture or nature? Is the freeing from sexual repression and thus, the exalting of the body over the mind, to blame? Or should we look to other factors that coincide with this new sexuality, and possibly are more causative of the distress that we witness in the teen, not only for the female but also for the male? Ponton describes a young 14-year-old boy, Jacob, who is six feet tall and highly developed for his age. He has been the subject of adult female advances by the stepmother of a friend, a substitute teacher, and adolescent girls who want his attention. Jacob still holds onto his childhood stuffed animals, and is overwhelmed by the sexual attention. What is there in our social mores that results in so much concentration and focus on sexuality? Ryder and Jetha (2014) indicate that too much preoccupation and time are focused on sex, and that while it is essential to our wellbeing, it is taken too seriously! As I have already questioned, is the selling of sexuality, the consumerization of sex, a means of deflecting an entire society from its most urgent issues: economic stability, eradication of poverty, equality of opportunity, the survival of the planet, and reduction of wars? Added to this are the problems of adequate child-care and education; we have an enormous number of issues that trouble our civilization!

The Enticing Patterns of Sex

The human body in twentieth-century ideology, according to Katz "was integrated into a new economy, and began more commonly to be perceived as a means of consumption and pleasure. . . ." (J.N. Katz, 1978). Bodies have become a commodity, a piece of conspicuous consumption that removes sex from a relationship, a connection between people, to a momentary satisfaction devoid of intimacy or plain human caring. One-night stands, now coined under the rubric of Hook-Ups, have become a rather commonplace mode of social interaction between men and women, women and women, and men and men. Social intercourse, increasingly dominated by the Internet, Facebook, Twitter, meeting rooms in which to chat and to engage in sexual orgies and even masturbatory sex, appear to transcend more intimate connections that involve a community, an ideology. Sexual pleasure tends to evaporate rather quickly with a stranger, and yet, as we shall see, it is becoming a dominant force in social relationships, especially with teenagers.

Ryan and Jetha (2014) indicate that monogamy for human beings is a "false" narrative, and that history bears this out, particularly in the twenty-first century. Sexual desires encompass more than what one object can provide, and require a vast number of exciting scenes. More money, according to *US News and World Report* (Ryan and Jetha, 2014) is spent on strip clubs than on Broadway theater, ballet, opera, and jazz clubs. Dossie Easton and Janet W. Hardy (1997), in their book *The Ethical Slut*, imbue sex, diverse sexual acts, the sexual experience with strangers, loved ones, dear friends, or casual relationships, with a sense of ecstasy. "Every orgasm is a spiritual experience . . . it integrates all parts of you in ecstatic consciousness." They also suggest that a spiritual awareness integrates the split between mind and body, and can create through the sexual experience a religious sense, a connection to "that divinity that always flows through you." (pp.37–38). They use the word *slut* to de-demonize the persons engaged in sex and sexual acts, not only in a monogamous relationship but even in the most casual encounters. There are a ". . . plethora of options for happy sluthood, from long-term 'vee triads, ' where two partners are sexual with one 'hud' partner but not with each other, to orgiastic recreational sex. . . ." (p.35) Thus, swinging, meetings in a bar, a plane, or a restroom can accompany a most exquisite form of sexuality, provided the twosome, threesome, or group sex participants are considerate and caring for all involved.

"*Sluts* celebrates sexuality with a person of any gender. . . . Sluts may choose to have solo sex or get cozy with the Fifth Fleet. . . . As proud sluts, we believe that sex and sexual love are fundamental forces for good, activities with the potential to strengthen intimate bonds, enhance lives, open spiritual awareness, even change the world. Furthermore, we believe that every consensual sexual relationship has these potentials and that any erotic pathway, consciously chosen and mindfully followed, can be a positive, creative force in the lives of individuals and their communities." (p.4)

I have made special note of this thinking, for I believe that it consciously expresses what perhaps lies in the unconscious of most people in their blissful wishes about sex. The dream of a utopian world in sexual relations, an end to fears, individual self-doubts, and the hunger for love and connection. Unfortunately, the reality for most in this rather libidinous culture has not been experienced with such a supreme and exquisite sense of spirituality and connection with the other.

Betty and John had a rather tempestuous relationship. They were part of a swinging group that met every weekend—a stable group that at times turned into some lasting sexual friendships. But, unfortunately, John broke the rules; he also had a penchant for prostitutes, for bondage sex, that left Betty out. This was intolerable for her and thus the marriage ended in divorce. Why was this so difficult for Betty? John loved her, she was the preferred one. Was it the exclusion that was intolerable, jealousy of the prostitute with whom she could not compete? Or did the prostitute illegitimatize the illusions that Betty gave to the sex act?

That I present this one example cannot in theory be considered a disclaimer to Easton and Hardy's assertion that sex can provide a community and individuals with a beatific feeling. An examination of the many cases given by other writers, as well as my own interviews, can provide some insight as to whether the unfreezing from repression of "free floating sex" has really benefited the individual and the culture. Or is it part of a conglomerate of forces that in fact are tending to destabilize the culture? Certainly, one can also suggest that these new forms of sexuality will lead to a different form of social organization. Foucault (1978) questioned: why has it been so arduous to break down the taboos against sex, to present sex as a truth, a knowledge of human living? He asked, "Had this knowledge become so costly, in political, economic, and ethical terms, that in order to subject everyone to its rule, it was necessary to assure them paradoxically, that their liberation was at stake?" Unfortunately, alongside with opening up the "sex book of knowledge" in the twenty-first century, we have also observed emotional repression. The contradictions lie in an increasing commercialization of sex, and an emotionality that is devoid of intrinsic human relatedness. We are witnessing a sexually provocative environment that dehumanizes the individual into a cookie-cutter figure of sexuality, a commodity to be bought.

Gail Sheehy's (2006) *Sex and the Seasoned Woman* has provided an interesting array of interviews that can help decipher the many dilemmas inherent in free and unfettered sex. Is it really a boon for the person and for the society? Carole, a 50-year old woman working in a doctor's office, tells a group of women about the delights of her sex life. She is divorced, and describes herself as "a big bubbly, fun-loving Jersey girl." She has a broad face, is about fifty pounds over the natural weight for her height, and would not be considered as the model of feminine sexuality that appears in advertisements. Her response to the forces of objectifying women is to claim that "If a man knows he's going to be pleasured, and you make sure he gets pleasure right away, he is not going to be grading you on your body shape. . . ." She further stated, "Men are really interested in your breasts and your butt." The two men she had been interested in rejected her; she is no longer interested in marriage but enjoys casual affairs or serial lovers.

It is possible to read Carole's words as an angry defense against men's superficial demands for physical beauty in women, and so has she become an unpaid "giver of pleasure" as a means to get men? Or can we discern in her behavior hostility and rage?—How shallow men's desire, if you just want marriage or a relationship with only a beautiful woman, I will give you a bit of sexual pleasure, but I have no respect for you, I mock you." Sheehy wonders why there is "so much traffic in the midlife singles bazaar"?

Dennis responds to Sheehy's question of what kind of woman men find attractive: " A beautiful blonde with a great body and who dresses well. You go from there to see if there's some chemistry and compatibility." Sheehy comments that this is "the stuff of fantasy," but unfortunately, it is this fantasy that dominates men's desires and women's frustrations. Let us recall that this is the era of women's liberation, and the belief that more basic human ideas compose the mental makeup of men and women.

Dennis, Carole, (not a couple) and friends spend many hours a week at singles' clubs looking to have a good time, and each hoping to meet someone special, to have a relationship. Most have been married before, and are either widowed or divorced. Casual sex occurs frequently, and the women are equally as assertive as the men. Sheehy notes that although the men are looking for beauty (a size ten), they still want to be taken care of, hovered over, and made to feel as though they are the sole support. They want the beautiful homemaker. The women want a companion, someone to share intimate thoughts and feelings with, and, equally important, they want a man who is a good lover, and who can take the lead sexually.

Sexting: For the Young

To those of us of the old-old generation sexting has a paradoxical quality; it appears to be a means of communicating with others but without much depth; it is so impersonal and sexualized that it defies comprehension. That the surprise at sexting rests with us "oldies" and not with the current generation is understandable. This is the time of great technology, sexual freedom, and experimentation. To display one's body on the cell phone to prove sexual appeal and prowess does not appear very different from the mass advertisements of three-quarter-nude bodies in seductive poses of both sexes. Sexting goes part and parcel with the technology of the twenty-first century, especially for the young. In past eras, *Penthouse* and *Playboy,* magazines considered risqué, but indeed mild by today's standards, were the secretive means of sexual titillation. The young were prohibited from buying the magazines partly due to the cost, meager by today's measure, but then out of the reach of most middle-class children, and especially the poor. Further, one feared getting caught by parents who would look morally askance at this prurient interest; and the rest of society's opprobrium that considered such sexual interests the prerogative of the adults, and mainly men.

Yet one of the difficulties in understanding the motivation in sexting is how it fosters a love or caring relationship between young persons, and I include homosexual and heterosexual youth. To what degree has the body overrun the nature of emotion, empathy, and thought-attraction, all of which tend to bind people, to form a bonding of individuals to one another? That sex is basic to survival of the species, and a means of individual pleasure, cannot override the importance of other human needs, such as real intimacy. Obviously, I have placed sexuality within the context of body and mind: a place of bodily satisfaction, human interaction, and emotional discourse—a place where we view raw appetite through the lens of controlled discharge of our sexual passions, by intertwining them with love, consideration, compassion, kindness, and pleasure. Perhaps I have over-estimated the individual's need for love and intimacy, and what is evolving is a new form of social and personal relationships.

And yet in our current emotional lexicon, to want to please a lover, even a young teenage lover, with your sexuality, your body, your looks, is a natural part of falling in love, especially adolescent love. But what are the motives behind sending nude or semi-nude pictures to total strangers, or those with whom there is no intimate relationship? One can only hypothesize that we have become a nation of exhibitionists, actors on a stage that require the praise and approval from an unknown audience. Is this sexting an indication of new forces in the society that help determine one's quality, one's self-worth by approval, that is, sexual admiration from total strangers or just acquaintances?

The book *Sexting* (2013) a compilation of papers from various educators, psychologists, and writers edited by Lauri S. Scherer, presents an interesting array of opinions on the meaning of sexting, and its impact on the health and welfare of both teens and the society. The editor's introduction notes that sexting is represented by a double standard. Girls who sext tend to be viewed as sluts and whores, while boys are viewed as studs, manly and desirable. Girls seem to be pressured by the boys to present themselves as sexual bodies, nude, half-nude, or in alluring postures, and if they don't comply they are referred to as frigid and rejected. Thus, sexting seems to have become an arena in which to prove oneself, to attain value, and at the same time, the very act of the teens' sexuality brings about shame and derision. The authors point to the suicide of a few girls, and a larger number that are bullied and humiliated, as a testament to the dangers inherent in sexting. It needs to be noted that most of the discourse concerns girls who are primarily induced to send sexy photos by the male. This leads one to question what is happening to the psyche of boys in this new social activity: what kind of men will they become; how kind, thoughtful, and considerate as lovers, fathers, and husbands? Other writers have indicated that the concern over sexting is exaggerated. Those who proclaim its dangers indicate that almost 20 percent of teens engage in sexting; those who contradict these numbers indicate that the statistics are inaccurate and that only about two percent indulge in sexting.

Mark, who just graduated from high school, thought that about half of the kids sexted. Personally, he felt no need to sext; it did not validate him. And further, he had a girlfriend, and though they discussed sex both felt that they would wait to have sexual intercourse. Getting good marks and sports were more import- ant. Was Mark in the minority or majority? He couldn't answer; though he recognized that about half of the kids in his high school, with a population of three thousand, probably have had sexual intercourse by the time they graduated, and a large majority of them have sexted.

Scherer (2013) also includes in this thoughtful compendium a number of issues that concern the civil liberties of the young, an appreciation for their sexuality, and at the same time an awareness of problematic mental health issues for the young created by sex- ting. Further, some papers stressed the need for parents and the school authorities to become more involved regarding the content and the effects of sexting; and perhaps even more important was the recognition that regardless of the exact numbers of students sexting, there is an inherent social issue that must be addressed. And that is the nature of brutality, and the mental anguish that is caused by this social media, sexting, that engages large numbers of people, especially the young. Just as a society needs to protect the young from physical abuse and neglect, so must a society pro- tect its young from mental and psychological abuse. Otherwise, we are in danger of cultivating a culture in which aggression is a dominant feature in individual and social relationships. Rushford Kidder commented, "Americans have let technology inform their morals and ethics, rather than letting their morals and ethics guide their use of technology" (p.97). Kidder is concerned that given society's "obsession" with sex, the failure to recognize the role of technology in this area is quite disappointing. He raised seven points as to why we as a society should be concerned with sexting. Aside from the legal dangers of "lewd and lascivious" behavior and transmission of child pornography, he was concerned as to its effects upon teenage pregnancies, too-early marriage and divorce, and the risks of creating more single-parent families. Further, he indicated his deep worry that sexting can lead to a culture of more rape, domestic abuse, and sexual predation. Kidder did not favor criminalization for sexting, but some means of protecting young people. He suggested that one way to curb or set limits on the contents of sexting was to design a program that will send a copy of the texted picture to a parent or guardian, or a third party for storage in an archive. This would give parents some control and ability to deal with the issue, and society a means of being alerted to possible predators. Certainly this method would raise issues with those who consider that the young have the right to their sexual privacy, out of the probing eyes of parents. Kidder also recognized this issue of privacy for teens and young adults, but the need to talk about sexting is imperative for the culture.

Hook-Ups: For the Young and the Old

Hook-ups connote a wide range of sexual activity from kissing, petting, oral sex, genital intercourse or anal sex with a person one has just encountered, or repeated hook-ups with the same person for primarily a sexual encounter. The implication in hook-ups is that there is no emotional entanglement or relationship. It has become the substitute for prostitution for the male, and a sense of freedom, a breaking of the bindings of sexual repression and inequality for the female.

Holly, a sophomore at a private East Coast college, was interviewed by Peggy Orenstein (2016) for her study of college students. She is bright, attractive and into hook-ups. Holly opposed the notion that sleeping around is only good for guys. She "feels accomplished" after she has sex "with someone that I wanted to have sex with." After sex the other night, her friends in the dorm gave her a "High Five," and " I felt accomplished just like a boy would.

I felt like, I went out, I looked good, I showed myself off, and I got it last night. Good for me." Was it simply the desire for sex, or was there some inner protest against the male-macho world that brags about its sexual conquests? It is possible to speculate that among the young we are witnessing a sexual war between women and men?—not really a revolution that is changing the way the sexes relate, but rather a way of not relating, a testing of power. If the guys can flaunt their sexual experiences, their hook-ups, so can I! Orenstein points out that today's young did not invent casual sex, but what has changed among college students, and increasingly in high school students, is that a relationship does not generally start with a date but rather with casual sex. The relationship may develop after the sexual act. Sex is not a product of intimacy, but has tended to become its precursor or at times its replacement. She quoted Debby Herbenick at Indiana University's Kinsey's Institute, who indicated that sex previously was common on college campuses, but now it has taken on an obligatory quality, "it's what you should be doing". She has talked to students who felt that "people ought to be able to have sex without any emotions, and if you can't then something is wrong with you." If this quality of casualness is desired, then what can we expect from the general interaction of people, the nature of friendships, and simply plain neighborliness? Can it be that the curtailment of emotions is the task for the twenty-first century? Certainly it makes it easier to divorce, to love people and leave them, and, perhaps even more frightening, to kill them.

It would be remiss to dismiss other theories that place high value on the liberation of sexuality from rigid morality or religious precepts. There are those who proclaim that free and un-moralized sexuality is necessary for the good of society. Pat Califia, (1994) in *Public Sex*, proclaimed "I am . . . bragging about my search for an ever more forbidden way to have an orgasm." Califia is a lesbian who also wishes to declare her public commitment to radical sex: to sadism and masochism. ". . . I do not simply mean sex, which differs from the 'norm' of heterosexual vanilla, male-dominated intercourse. But being a sex radical means being defiant as well as deviant." It appears that the need to free sexuality from social repression has also taken on the form of declaring the most private aspects of sexual life in the public forum. One can wonder how much of this is activated by political necessity to remove sexual restrictions and taboos from the sometimes cruel arm of culture. Or are we dealing, in parallel, with a powerful exhibitionistic trend in society?

Homosexuality

I have included homosexuality in this study of sexual patterns, marriage, and infidelity. As a group defined by their choice of a sexual object, they represent an important component in American culture. The nature of this group's sexual behavior also reflects on family stability, intimate relationships between individuals, and the level of fidelity among married couples. Legalized marriage between same-sex couples exists in 37 states plus the District of Columbia. This legalization of a relationship reflects the prevailing attitude regarding the meaning of marriage as a socially recognized institution; and, therefore, fidelity and adultery impact marriage. It is necessary to make a distinction between fidelity and adultery, as changes in the institution of marriage are occurring in which couples may be faithful to each other in love and commitment, but engage in sexual relationships with others, or have established polyamorous relationships. This, as I have already indicated, applies to both heterosexual and homosexual relationships. Thus, it is possible to be faithful in a polyamorous or open marriage relationship, provided there is honesty and mutual agreement.

Ruth Houston (2002), in her article on Life/Relationships/Sex and Relationships," quoted a statistic indicating that in 80% of all marriages, hetero-and homo-sexual, and committed relationships, at least "one form or another" of infidelity occurred. In homosexual relationships, married or committed, 100% of all the couples experienced infidelity within the first five years of the relationship. Couples who stayed together over ten years accepted the painful realities of infidelity, and more than 85% reported that the biggest difficulty in the relationship resulted from the problems around infidelity. What then do these statistics indicate? The capacity to remain monogamous or faithful appeared to be difficult for all, regardless of sexual orientation, age, race, and economic levels.

Sexual Promiscuity in Bohemian Life

There was no secret about open sex in the early Bohemian life of Greenwich Village, the Bloomsbury group in England of Virginia Woolf, or various Utopian societies that attempted alternate forms of living and loving arrangements. Elizabeth Abbott (2016), in her book *Mistresses*, recounts the stories of well-known men and women who were guilty of flaunting sexual mores: a single mistress, a multitude of sexual partners, several mistresses, and women who themselves were mistresses and had man lovers simultaneously. Note that the title of the book is *Mistresses*, a guilty term for a woman in our social lexicon. And not a guilty man, for there isn't a comparable term for the man, and thus, he becomes a lover, a rather disingenuous term for his sexual forays. The book deals with flagrant women who were married, took male lovers with great passion, and had both simultaneous and sequential lovers. There was Mistress Catherine Walston, who was the lover of the writer Graham Greene, and of other men simultaneously. Harry Walston, her husband, knew of all the affairs, and at times he consented to their meetings and sleeping arrangements, and at other times limited the relationships. George Eliot, the great English writer, born Mary Ann Evans, was madly in love with George Lewes, a married man whose wife had delivered their first child by her lover, Thomas Hunt. Lillian Hellman, the gifted American playwright, and Dashiell Hammett, writer of mystery books, seared their *strum-und-drang* through the literary community, known both for its non-conformity and its passions of love, hate, and revenge. Theirs was a relationship of many decades. There is Héloïse, the woman philosopher, and Abelard, the cleric; their tale was one of great passion, love, heartache, and religious conflict. And Salinger, the lauded writer of *Catcher In the Rye*, (an elderly man, a lover of young girls) and Joyce barely out of her nubile age, engaged in sex, love, cruelty and repentance, and extrasexual affairs. Most confusing of all was the love affair between Hannah Arendt and Martin Heidegger; she a great Jewish philosopher, writer and teacher, and he a brilliant, world-renowned philosopher, and a Nazi. He was married when they met, and began their affair while she was his student. The deep love continued through his multiple affairs, her various marriages and love trysts, and most notably, through the reality of his support for Hitler and Nazi ideology, that led to the destruction of millions of Jews and non-Jews. How to account for the power of love and sex that even flouts an individual's basic morality and ethics?

What Will It Be Like?

As we have ended the twentieth century with amazement and awe at the technological brilliance that surrounds us, and have entered into the twenty-first century with perhaps equal amazement at all the varieties of sexual attitudes and behavior, will this be an age of discovery of new kinds of sexual mores to match the technological gateway? Or shall we discover that our sexual relationships, marriage, monogamy, adultery, and betrayals resonate with past periods of history that were likewise influenced by social upheavals, wars, migrations, power struggles, and instability? Is it possible that the Emperor still has no clothes, and we appear as naked in our sexuality as the Emperor? Margaret Mead's optimism that the new trends in society will make claim to the older moralities on love, and marriage will again emerge, appears more as a wish than a reality: "The old certainties of the past are gone, and everywhere there are signs of an attempt to build a new tradition, which, like the old traditions that have been cast aside, will again safely enfold growing boys and girls, so that they may grow up to choose each other, marry, and have children." Yet, Mead, I suspect, would have been rather surprised to view this new world of polyamory, casual hook-ups, and the number of single-parent families, mostly women, struggling for existence. One wonders if multiple loves or polyamorous sex is really the road to a blissful life? In the end, the boredom and ennui, the curse of monogamy, will also flare up in infidelities and adulterous relationships. But, perhaps hope burns eternal, and so fatasies push us onwards.

Chapter Eight
Divorced Men and Women

The divorce rate is very high in the western world and more particularly in the United States.

Within five years of marriage, the anticipated divorce rate is 20 percent. After ten years of marriage, the divorce rate is 33 percent. For the young between the ages of 22–30, remarriage is not difficult, nor is finding another partner for either sex. But for women over 45, it is a more difficult task (Travernise, 2011).

Men of 45 and more remarry or find partners without difficulty. The man of middle age is no longer interested in consorting with a woman his own age. He generally seeks a younger woman. This is not new to society.

In past centuries, the average length of marriage lasted from 16–18 years. This was the result of poor health conditions and the early demise of partners. The average life expectancy was 47 years. Death in childbirth was a common phenomenon for women. Thus, multiple marriages for those persons who lived beyond the age of 45 were not uncommon, as demise was the reprieve from long marriages and boredom. Divorce is the present-day equivalent of shortened relationships due to death, and the ability to satisfy the urge for newness. Today the average life expectancy is 76 years. A healthy, vibrant population strives for multiple experiences and sexual pleasure. In the wake of increased financial security, people want to optimize their worldly resources. There is a long list of pleasurable play in multiple sexual relationships. There is also an increase in divorce in the older population: the sixty- and seventy-year olds who are dissolving the bonds of matrimony .

Current society appears to be in flux. Men are caught between the impulse to seek ever new and thrilling gratification and the emotional needs of belonging and security. They believe they can find paradise in a new partner when the old one fails to live up to the fantasy. The media image of pin-up girls, sexy blondes, big-busted, with narrow waist, curved hips, and long lean legs, has been part of men's mental portfolio since early adolescence. A real-life woman fails miserably in comparison. How much do these fantasy images influence the real-life relationship between men and women? Are these external images, these pin-ups, responsible for creating an unreal picture of what women are really like? Or do these pin-up images reflect an underlying basic fantasy that is responsible for the creation of the pin-up? Why is physical beauty such a driving force, especially since the real world is a mixture of beauty and imperfection?

In reality, most women do not live up to the fantasy images of men or the standards that the movies, TV, or magazines display, and most men are not married to models or beauty types. How much does the discrepancy between fantasy, cultural stereotypes, and basic reality impinge on the problems that couples face in a marriage? Is the search for beauty a driving force behind infidelity for the man? The multitude of magazines and articles that instruct women on beauty tips and control of weight have created an excessive consciousness regarding looks. Billeon and Ray J *(Death Of the Cheating Man)* give instructions to men on what clothes to don from dress-up garb to sleepwear, in order to be sexually attractive to women. Younger women, even teenagers, have become the model of sexuality, thus what opportunity exists for older women in this highly eroticized culture? How much emotional energy and involvement with looks is demanded so that women can comply with the cultural standard? Unfortunately, it is a standard that ignores the richness of inner life, and tends to make plastic people. Emotional rapport, understanding, values, and common interests have little to do with the images of a partner portrayed by the culture. So how do we reconcile the picture of a beautiful woman that each and every man should have with what is real and what is possible? How much is ones self-esteem, both male and female, affected by the pin-up image?

Jim, a teacher in his middle fifties, is divorced and would like to remarry. He wonders at men who are with unattractive women. He hates himself for these thoughts but can't help it; he wants a beautiful and shapely woman.

Stephanie was anorectic as an adolescent. She remembers feeling the power of control that she exercised over food. It was the one thing that she felt was within her ability to control; it was her body. She denied any thoughts of looks or sex as a motive for the anorexia. As an adult she rails against the culture that demands thinness for women, that makes them so weight-conscious and so preoccupied with exercise. Stephanie is petite, thin and very attractive. She hates men who are concerned with looks, decries them as being superficial, and feels that men want to subjugate women. All women think about is looks and trying to please a man. Stephanie is very concerned with food and exercise. The very thing she deplores in other women and in men operates in her own psyche. Since it is so intolerable a state for her, she must shut off the recognition of how the demand of good looks influences her, and can see it only in others.

Lisa fluctuates between slenderness and overweight. She is on psychotropic drugs, and the medication results in the weight gain, but so does her overeating. She is incensed whenever one of the numerous psychiatrists she has visited for medication refer to her weight, and tell her lose weight, or decide on a medication depending on weight factors.

Despite one's own judgment that invalidates the cultural norms, it is very difficult to eradicate the power of images as to the beautiful woman and the successful male. Honesty and reality are in constant conflict with our culture.

Chapter Nine
The Single Mother, Children and Sex

You are divorced. You are between 35 and 50, and your children are very young or are teenagers. You are human; you want male companionship and a sexual relationship.

You are enlightened, but you know that to have sexual relationships with a man who is not the father of your children in your home is problematic. Perhaps you believe that the reasons stem from a religious or social moral code. You would like to be free of the restrictions, but you are unable to free yourself. And if you have, somehow it is a disaster. Either you could not enjoy it, or he had difficulties, and then life with and for your children, regardless of age, became very difficult.

So what is the problem? Young children, of course, have no knowledge of sex. That is what you would like to believe. Awareness about sex does not begin until—what age—8, 9, 10? You try to convince yourself that the 3, 4, 5, 6-year old is an innocent lamb. (Freud, 1905) Thus, you should be able to have the boyfriend or lover sleep over in the same bed.

The conception that young children are sexually ignorant is a myth. They do not have the adult level of understanding, but their heads are full of imaginative ideas, and they have constructed their own concepts of what occurs between a man and a woman in the bed. It is very sexual, and they are very stimulated by their ideas and the reality of what goes on between a man and a woman.

One of the major events in a child's development is that he/she must come to grips with the sexual relationship between mother and father. Children are included in almost every aspect of the parental relationship. The secrets of the bedroom, the closed door, and the intimacy of the sexual relationship are closed to them.

Lizzie, age 5, announces loudly at the end of her kindergarten day, as her father is buttoning her coat, "Daddy, I am going to sleep with you." Daddy turns red and utters not a word. It is not an easy adjustment for children who wish to be the center of the parental world, but it is a reality that, ultimately, they must accept. Psychologically, children must accept that the sexual relationship between the parents excludes them. They cannot have what mother or father have with each other. They cannot make the babies that mother and father make. They cannot be substitute lovers for their parents. It is a hard blow to the child's ego. Rivalries and jealousy of the parent are common. These feelings give way in time to the development of their own skills and new knowledge about the world of things that engage them. Gratifications in life, especially the loving relationship with both parents, are excellent substitutes for the prohibitions they encounter (Galenson & Roiphe, 1981). When there is a divorce, something catastrophic happens in the child's world. The child, once protected by both parents from the harsh realities of the world, now faces an emotional upheaval. Divorce catapults all of the unconscious sexual and aggressive feelings that had been peacefully hidden away to the surface. In the child's mind, old wishes begin to emerge; he/she is the preferred one, he /she feels the victor over the same-sex parent; he/she is guilty for the divorce. These childhood fantasies are shattered by the confrontation with the parent's new sexual life. The child must confront other rivals for the parent's attention and affection. Either father or mother has other love interests—one or many. Each new friend of the parent is a potential rival. What if the new friend has children? The world is bleaker, more fraught with rivals and disappointments (Wallerstein, 2004).

What role does sex play in the child's thoughts and emotions in this atmosphere? There is heightened sexual curiosity and pre-occupation with sexuality. We would like to deny these facts, but just listen closely to children's remarks and/or observe how their behavior changes.

Jennifer was a delightful little girl of 7. Her parents separated and both began relationships with others. When her mother dat-ed, Jennifer was sent to stay at her aunt's house for the evening. She became irritable, obstreperous, and even hit her mother in a rage. She wanted to get her period, and daily checked her panties anticipating its arrival. Poor Mama! What a dilemma!

What was Jennifer reacting to? The loss of an integrated family? The security of both parents as a daily source of consistent support and love was no longer an assured quantity. Both parents had other interests that excluded her. Further, it is not possible for Mama to join the dating scene and remain as involved with the minute details of daily life, especially the finite details of her child's life, as formerly. The focus of family life subtly and unalterably changes when there is a divorce or separation. Jennifer was reacting to the changes but, more significantly, she was reacting to intruders in her love life with her parents. These strangers had little to offer her. She was scared, and she was angry.

Divorce leads to family disintegration, to a reduction in adult authority and protection. The parent of custody, generally the mother, is burdened, emotionally and very frequently by financial stress. Demands from the family are greater when one individual carries the main responsibility. Once a woman is divorced, her income level is markedly reduced. She has to handle school, medical, and all the responsibilities connected with child care. Emotionally, it is no longer possible to be so attuned to the nuances of her child's needs and to respond with the same degree of emotional and physical energy. What happens to the child when she is away from home, when she has to work, to shop, go to the doctor, and have a little recreation outside of the home?

What about the woman's need for love, affection, and sex? How to balance children and another relationship? Even in the best of circumstances, when the male companion is very understanding, the difficulties are enormous. Where to put the man to sleep? If the man stays over he is fortunate to sleep in the bed downstairs— Susie age 13, still manages to have a bellyache at night and wants to sleep in Mama's bed. And Mama had better be in that bed and not in the one downstairs. What if there is no room, no separate bed—what to do? So, you go to his house, and if you are lucky, the kids go to grandma or the aunt's house—but how often? Once a week—that's ok when you are just dating, but what happens when there is a relationship? If the man is separated or divorced and his wife has custody, he is a free agent. To begin a new relationship with a person encumbered burdens him. He wants to escape the burdens, having already left a difficult relationship. It is not an easy situation for either the woman or the man.

Betty asks, "What do you think if I send Dana across the street to my friend's house? I met this man and I am falling in love. I need to have time to explore the relationship. He lives an hour-and-a-half away. I worry. Dana and I are getting along fine now, you know how terrible she was for months." Betty has been separated for 8 months. She began to date immediately, and though Dana rarely met the men, she knew Mama was dating. Was it the separation that caused Dana to become a difficult child? Was she expressing her pain and fear through anger, a much easier emotion for children to tolerate? How much did Mama's dating contribute to the difficulties? She was in danger of another loss—her mother to some strange man. Would this man love her; would she love him—and then, what about her father? Would she betray him by loving another man? What kind of sexual fantasies went through Dana's mind? What was her mother doing with this man—kissing, touching each other—would a baby come? We can assume that all played a role, and when Mama stopped dating for a while things got better.

I do not wish to moralize. Separation and divorce are devastating for both partners and for children. Yet, the woman bears the brunt of child care and financial and social difficulties. She is entitled to a private love life. The cost is high—children are distraught, they make life difficult for the mother, and she is caught in a Catch-22.

We cannot forget that infidelity plays a significant role in divorce. Betty's husband was having affairs. She wanted to find a man who would love her, and only her. She did not want to be alone. She wanted to feel desired as a woman, and to have a satisfying sexual life. She wanted to be a good mother. Betty loved her daughter. Dana was her world; she worried about her schooling, her music and art lessons; she wanted the best for Dana. If only Betty could deny that her dating affected Dana, then maybe she would be more relaxed. Unfortunately, as much as Betty tried to escape the knowledge that her dating was affecting Dana, she had to face the truth. Dana or her? It is an untenable position for the woman.

Rebecca knew that Richard was interested in other women. They could not walk out of the house together without his interest in her dissipating. His speech faltered, and his eye roved over every female body. Yet it took a number of years for her to face the truth that he also slept with other women. In spite of three young children, she could not go on with the marriage. Of course, there were other issues that made the relationship untenable, but his infidelity, his indiscretion, were too much to bear. Yet he would not leave; he refused to separate. When he finally agreed to leave, Rebecca felt an enormous sense of relief. She did not want another involvement. Dating, having a sexual relationship was fine. There was no conflict about a man's staying over; it would never happen. The children would not have to be conflicted or jealous. They only had to share her with work. All her spare time was with the children.

Richard quickly established relationships with women, some casual, some more serious, and finally he remarried. The children spent Saturdays with him and occasional weekends. What did they see, what did they know? Jason, the youngest, did not have as much difficulty, as each woman friend became his friend. He would bake bread with them, chat, and generally enjoyed the attention. Robert, who was the oldest child, had little to do with his father; he stayed away. Claire, the middle child and sole daughter, was acutely jealous. Her interest in boys piqued. She would go to their houses without parental permission. She flaunted her mother's authority, lied and stole from her mother. At her father's wedding, she insisted on a long white gown. If she could not be the bride, at least she would match her. In relation to her father, she was a good girl, obedient and always trying to please him. For a long time, she felt like her father's favorite child, certainly preferred over her mother. Richard's remarriage was a blow to her ego. She had lost in the competition, but still she felt that she had been victorious over her mother.

Claire experienced her mother as an undesirable woman, a loser. Unfortunately, her father encouraged this perception, and his constant attacks on her mother heightened Claire's overestimated sense of herself. This sense of self-esteem was based on the fantasy that she was better than her mother. The fantasy did not carry her very far in relation to boys and girls her own age. She became promiscuous with boys, thinking to conquer them with sex, only to be used and thrown away. She soon found that girls were formidable rivals; they had a good sense of self and were more adept with their competitive styles.

Would these misfortunes have occurred if Rebecca had not

divorced Richard? There is no telling answer. What we can assume is that the father's multiple girlfriends certainly had to aggravate Claire's rivalry with women, and contributed to her sense of inadequacy. Further, did it help that Rebecca hid her men friends, or did it distort Claire's perception of her mother as a loser, and thus, create an illusion of Claire's superiority? The struggle to function responsibly as a divorced parent is difficult. The social structure is not supportive, and the extended family is generally scattered. Men, unfortunately, are not sufficiently attuned to the needs of the woman's children or the woman's concern about her children. Sex looms large in our culture and often precedes a relationship. The dilemma is too often between sex, a relationship, or aloneness. To love one's children should not require the sacrifice of one's personal life. Unfortunately, when there is divorce or separation, conflict between one's sexual desires and the psychological wellbeing of children emerges. Single parents are frequently in a no-win situation. The valid demands and needs of children require restraint and restriction in their sexual and emotional lives. Divorce may remove one set of problems, but where children are concerned, a new set of difficulties emerges. Divorce is relatively easy to obtain. The legal restraints are not arduous. Society is accepting; no longer is "divorcée" a pejorative term. What has been achieved in the legal and social systems cannot alleviate the suffering that divorce, infidelity and adultery has caused in the personal and emotional world.

Chapter Ten
Interviews:
The Reality of Love Gone Astray

Case One: JANE

Jane, age 57, is an attractive, trim woman with black curly hair, cut in a soft bob. There is tension in her face and her sad eyes belie the big smile with which she greets me.

She tries very hard to hide her distress, but her mannerisms and stiff actions convey another meaning. She is holdng a letter in her hand and with a sudden motion places the envelope in front of me.

No word—silence—as I glance at the envelope and then open it.

My shock is apparent as I read the note.

"Your husband is having an affair with Gloria. Everyone knows about it—so you should know it too."

A heartless message, anonymous, not very literate. I blurt out; "Do you think it was the woman who sent this?" She had thought of this, but concluded that it was probably her husband., as she had compared the letters and numbers and some matched his handwriting.

She had been in a state of shock. The woman was a whore; she worked with him. It was known that she slept with everyone. (She was not a whore in the literal sense, but a woman who is promiscuous in this day and age is still considered a prostitute).

Men friends had told her that she offered herself to a group of them as they sat around the lunch table. She would give them the "best blow job" that would send them over the hill.

How could her husband go with the likes of this woman: not pretty, in fact ugly, on drugs, alcoholic, snorting coke—what was he thinking?

When she confronted him with the note, he did not deny it—he simply stated that he was involved with her as a friend but there was no sex. He moved out the next day. He claims to have his own apartment but Jane is sure he is living with her.

Had there been any warnings, any signs? She was a little suspicious: he was never home. That was not unusual, as he was a workaholic.

He was not a sociable man and preferred work; he was not interested in people or in socializing. He would come home and watch television. He hardly talked, and she had little idea as to what was going on with his business or what he thought about. Her friends did not like to go out with him, as his silences and moods were unpleasant. He developed a pattern of coming home very late, eating dinner, and watching television. Lately, he had become meaner. He began to eat in front of the television set, leaving her alone at the dinner table.

Sex had decreased in the last few years. She wasn't that interested. She had lost interest after her menopause. She was vaginally dry and had a bad reaction to lubricants. But, he too, seemed less interested in sex. She was not adverse to oral sex, and she tried to satisfy him orally. Surprisingly, on their last vacation together, he had been pleasant and more affectionate. Though a strange thing happened on this vacation: he had wanted her to go to a sex club. In spite of her reservations, she was willing to go with him, until she learned that they were meeting another couple whom he met on the Internet in the "chat room." "I could not go through with it." This couple was into switching. He promised that nothing would happen. She knew that for the last few years he had been into chat rooms. "I guess he was changing, but I just could not face it."

Would she have left him after receiving the note if he didn't want to leave? No, not at that time. Not until financially things had improved. "I would have waited until I was ready. Still, I didn't do badly; I got the house and an apartment in Arizona."

"After this happened, I felt too ashamed to leave the house, to go to the grocery store. I felt that every one knew; they would look at me with pity and talk about me. I wondered what was wrong with me. This was a second marriage. The first hadn't worked out. My first husband stopped having sex with me. I never knew why or what the problem was. We went for counseling to a minister who advised me to leave him." No explanations were given, and to this day she has no idea of what the problem was. "My two daughters are from my first marriage. He was a fairly good father and we remained friends. My second husband did not show much interest in the children. I guess as a stepfather, he didn't feel responsible. The kids grew up OK; they did well at school, had friends, and are now happily married. Their father died about ten years ago."

Jane continued: "I left my family and friends to move to this area. I have a few friends, but life in this town has always been lonely. People are not very friendly. I worked for a long time and helped support us while Jack was building the business. In the last few years, I stopped work. Most of the time I was home alone, and in the summer spent a good deal of time working in the garden. During the winter months, I would go to Arizona, and he would come down for a few weeks.

I am not interested in meeting anyone but if a nice man came along, I would not reject him. It wasn't a great marriage, but I did not want to break it up. One divorce was enough. Before we were married, things were much better. The sex was good, and we had good times together. Once we all moved in together, things changed; perhaps it was the kids. We no longer had the same privacy. He never complained, but he was rarely home."

Lives of quiet despair! Jane and her husband rarely fought. There was little talk between them; and I suspect that emotionally she dared not face the distance in their lives or the emptiness that she experienced. She was already traumatized by one broken marriage; the sense of sexual rejection by her first husband weighed too heavily on her to face a second rejection. Intellectually, she could not let herself think about the meaning of Jack's behavior. She simply lived day-to-day, not questioning, isolated and depressed. There were no friends to talk to, of whom to emotionally reverberate. Her family, parents and siblings lived about an hour's distance from her home. She visited them, loved them, but never shared her distress until after the separation. She worked, raised her children, and kept the house, maintaining a high level of functioning but with a very heavy heart. A remarkably stoic life!

Case Two: HILLARY

Hillary is a slight woman with gray hair that once glimmered with shades of golden red. She is pretty, with a perky face and rather shy demeanor, but there is a wicked gleam in her eye. Her quietness belies a rather savvy woman, a retired law professor in her mid-sixties.

She talked quietly about her betrayal by her husband, some 25 years ago, almost musing on it, and thinking thoughts she had never considered before our interview. I could tell that, despite her spoken wish, she permitted remembrances that were not pleasant, and ideas that she had never wanted to consider.

I kept wondering what had she felt then and now on reflection; what was the real emotion? She talked as though it were a story that had happened to another person; perhaps that was the result of time and forgetfulness. I had to be careful not to put my feelings into her emotions.

Hillary had married a man 12 years her senior from a very different background and religion. Her parents had disapproved; her mother felt that he was not genuine. But she was madly in love; he was debonair, good-looking, and fun. It was not that she had no boyfriends; there were always men in her life, but they were her age, boys, and he was a man. So, against her parents' wishes, she married; they went off to Bermuda, with no wedding ceremony, and no parents, just the two of them, quietly marrying. Life initially was happy: he had a good job in industry and she was a beginning attorney. Life seemed like a big party, with vacations, many friends, nothing to disturb their relationship. Six years into the marriage, they had a son. Things started to change, imperceptibly. He started to come home later, but she thought nothing of it. Then he began to drink; he became alcoholic; perhaps, he had always been one, but it had not been evident. She became distressed with his behavior, he had a terrible temper and she was frightened of him. He never hit her but his angry, violent moods were hard to take. She never thought that he was having an affair; it just didn't occur to her until one night in his sleep he called out a woman's name and she asked if he was having an affair. He denied it, but it became evident to her that there was another woman. The drinking, the lateness, the emotional storms went on for about a year, at which point she suggested separation. He seemed very relieved and then admitted to having another woman. He subsequently married the woman.

It was not the affair that troubled her; it was his drinking and behavior. In retrospect, she believes that he was torn between herself and the other woman and that this was at the root of his drinking. She could have tolerated the affair; of course, he would have had to give up the other woman. They never talked about what went wrong in the marriage, even though they have remained on friendly terms. Is it that she denied her own curiosity? Or were there things about herself that she did not want to hear?

Though she did not volunteer the information, at my asking, she admitted that she had had an affair during the marriage. It was with a colleague, a fling, nothing serious. This was during the period when there were parties, and switching, but not at the parties. People were more discreet. She was sure that most of her friends had had affairs. Perhaps her husband even had an affair with the wife of the man that she was sleeping with. If so, it would not have bothered her. It was all an ego trip, pleasurable to think that men found you attractive. Now, it was no longer important to me.

In her current marriage, she could have had an affair. A friend was pursuing her but it seemed like too much effort, and she didn't want to take a chance of causing any difficulties in the marriage. She had some suspicion that her husband may have had an affair. She was angry and confronted him, but he denied it. She would not break up the marriage over it, unless it had continued. She was not devastated, just angry. But she got over it and the marriage is a good one. They have had their ups and downs; nothing is perfect.

Hillary is cool, even-tempered, and emotionally noncommittal. The juxtaposition of her affair during the first marriage and her husband's drinking and subsequent affair leaves no impression. There was no reflection on the possibility that he may have been responding to her affair, though it was never talked about or acknowledged. How interesting that people could be "swingers," sleeping around and pretending that it did not bother them or their partner. Hillary's husband Jack became an alcoholic and started an affair with a woman whom he later married. Twenty five years later, with a good bit of life experience, a second marriage, and anger at her current husband's possible affair, she seemed to have little awareness as to the emotional consequences of her own adulterous act or adultery in general.

I wonder why Hillary did not even conceive of the possibility that her sexual affair could have impacted on her husband, and could have driven Jack into his affair. This is a possibility, not a statement of fact. The striking element in the interview was Hillary's failure to acknowledge her own affair. She related it only when asked. Was this withholding an attempt to deny that she had done something that could have been very disturbing to Jack? Was Jack's behavior a reaction to her betrayal? There was never any mention of her affair; was it possible that Jack could not deal with the rejection, the humiliation, directly and thus acted out with drinking and women?

Hillary focused on Jack's betrayal when she probably was the first to start the sexual affairs. For Hillary it was a sexual fling; for Jack, his affair was a romance, a secure partner. Perhaps guilt and denial operate to obscure the meaning and impact of one's behavior. Not to think is not to know; and thus guilt and pain are hidden, driven to the distant arenas of psychic life.

Case Three: MARIANNE

Marianne is a physician in her fifties, tall, with fine chiseled features and hair pulled back; she has the look of a Greek goddess. Her eyes flashed as she related the tale of her husband's betrayal. In truth, they were not legally married but considered themselves such, and introduced each other as husband and wife. They did not feel it necessary to legalize the relationship, as both had previous marriages, and there were a number of children from their marriages. He had had two previous marriages; she had one. Though the breakup had occurred 15 years ago, and she has subsequently remarried, her remembrance had the quality of yesterday.

Their relationship seemed ideal; he, too, was a physician. They had so much in common, wonderful friends, a lovely home, and interesting work. She had no idea that he was having an affair; to this day she can't quite believe it. They were always together, except when they attended separate conferences. She knew that Ruth was at one of the conferences, as he mentioned having dinner with her. Ruth and I were somewhat friendly; we were physicians at the same hospital and occasionally lunched together.

"I can't believe that he married her, she is so unattractive and old looking. What could she give him that I didn't?" mused Marianne. Their sex life was wonderful, though she suddenly remembered that he started to complain that she did not satisfy him. That was a surprise, as he always said that the sex was good. There were other signs, but they seemed so petty. He began to complain that she was not intellectual enough. She scoffed at this, as they had been together for seven years, they went to the theater, the opera, ballet, and she wrote many papers for medical journals; she ascribed this to some rivalry on his part. Certainly Ruth has not achieved the level of success that Marianne had but, of course, Ruth is a rich woman. For the first time it dawned on Marianne that maybe Mark had left her for the money.

She could not fathom his leaving her; she was devastated. "Do you know how he left me? He just called on the phone and said, ' I am not coming home anymore, and I am leaving you.' The next day he came and took his clothes. A few months later, he moved in with Ruth.

"I was distraught. I could not function for several weeks. Friends came and stayed with me; they would call every morning and evening to see how I was. I could barely go to work. I would come home and collapse on the bed. The hurt, the confusion, I had no idea; no sense of what went wrong. It was the worse time of my life."

How was her previous marriage? Well, her husband was also having an affair, but she did not realize it until her therapist pointed it out to her. She was not too distressed by this, as the marriage was not a very satisfying one for her. The sex was not good, and she was not very respectful of him. She felt intellectually superior. She stayed in the marriage for the sake of her daughter. She understood his relationship with the other woman, whom he then married. The woman respected him and really loved him; they are still together.

In the course of the interview, I asked if she had any affairs in her first marriage. Somewhat chagrined, she admitted to having numerous affairs, and one that lasted three years. She had been in love with the other man but would not marry him. He had divorced his wife, expecting to marry her. She felt he was not stable; there was mental illness in his family and subsequently, he committed suicide.

The degree of pain and rage she expressed at Mark's betrayal, the emotional distress, still consumed her. She could not forgive him and, more telling, she still had no idea why he really left her. Could it have been simply for the money? We will never know, as they never talked about their relationship once he left. He refused to talk to her.

Is it possible that there were no obvious clues, that Mark was probably having an affair with Ruth, and that he had left telltale signs around? Hillary's pain, distress and devastation are in no way assuaged by the memories of her own infidelities. The pain we inflict on others lies within another mental sphere than the pain we receive. Human beings have the capacity to isolate pain inflicted from pain received, and psychically the connection does not serve as a mitigating force against the ravages of betrayal.

Case Four: BRENDA

Brenda, small, petite, with an ingenuous smile, approached me in the lobby of a hotel with an "I-am-going-to-knock-you-over quality with my tale of betrayal." And indeed she did! After three-quarters of an hour interview, I was told that she had never married the father of her child, nor had she ever married, nor did she wish to. She was running with her libido, she would sleep with whomever she wanted from 25 to 70. I wondered if this was her revenge on all men for their betrayals.

Brenda, now aged 42, is a secretary for a vice president in a corporate firm in a small Northeastern town. She never attended college but has taken many college courses. Clearly, she is a very clever lady. Brenda was madly in love with Charles. She was 19 years old. He was tall, handsome and suave. They were going to marry, and had even set the date. She became pregnant, and he did not want the child; he wanted her to have an abortion. Though she was Catholic, this was not the reason for going on with the pregnancy. She wanted the baby. They had been living together. She then discovered that he was having an affair with her brother's friend's sister. At first he denied it but finally admitted the truth. With a smile, she relates her fury. When she gave birth, she did not allow him to take her to the hospital and would not allow him to visit her. He was running around by then with other women, but finally settled on Rita, the first of the women. Charles had little to do with his daughter, and refused to pay child support. He finally moved with Rita to Florida, where they married and had four children. Eventually, they moved back to her area. The nerve! They wanted to move into an apartment that faced her windows.

She has no idea why he would not marry her. His brother called her a whore (the gall) when he and his lot were all running around with women. She was faithful to Charles; she had no interest in other men.

Her life has been her daughter, a beautiful young woman now attending graduate school. She feels she did a wonderful job raising Glenda, except where men were concerned. She has not taught her how to choose wisely, and her boyfriends turn out to be womanizers like her father. "But, she has brains and will do all right."

Brenda has no wish to marry; there have been men who wanted to marry her, but she has refused—they can't be trusted, and she even saw one of them with another woman while they were still involved. "So how can you trust a man?" Of course she made no connection with the fact that she refused to marry him, and, perhaps, he may have felt rejected and was seeking a more secure partner. Yet, maybe her evaluation was correct. Is it possible that Brenda chooses men who are habitually unfaithful; is there some unconscious pattern that draws her to a particular male?

Interestingly, she and Charles have remained friends: they "sleep together."

She tells me this with a grin, like a naughty girl or a woman who defies convention. He is divorced, but even when he was still married to Rita, they would sleep together. She owes Rita no loyalty; after all, she went with Charles knowing that Charles was with her, and she was pregnant. All rules are off, no obligations.

She denied that she was afraid to be hurt again: no fears, just men can't be trusted. Same with all her girlfriends: the men cheated on them. She gets together with a group of women every few months and they share their sexual experiences. They have had it with men—no deep involvement, enough hurt and betrayal. They can play the same game as the men.

She appears elated as she talks, laughing, in control, but do I catch an undercurrent of sadness? I ask, "are you sad", and then she confesses, "Sometimes I cry in the shower, never in front of people, I never let my daughter see me in tears. My daughter is what I live for!"

What has made this feisty woman into a man-eater? She takes her sexual pleasures; her sexual desires are strong. She wants no emotional attachments. There does not appear to be any rancor in her voice. I hear plain pleasure at the conquests. Even sleeping with her former lover, the father of her daughter, has the ring of conquest. She acts like the stereotype of men—adulterers, profligates, simply out for a good time sexually. She denies revenge against Charles, who has come to typify all men. Her refusal to marry speaks to an undercurrent of deep distrust in men. What is the source? She had a close relationship with her mother. Her parents were divorced, though her father adored her mother. He was alcoholic and this broke up the marriage. She became the adulterous man/woman; since she could no longer trust herself, she certainly could not trust another man. She did not hate men; she enjoyed conquering them, a form of behavior we usually associate with the male. She blamed the man for not permitting her to be a woman. She could be a mother but not a feminine wife. Therein, lay Brenda's pain, a deep deprivation. She would never have the companionship of a man as either husband or father for her child.

Case Five: LESLIE

Leslie, age 77, a retired college professor, medium height, brown hair, with rather sad blue eyes, reminisces about the past. There is regret in her voice, and she conveys a sense of wishing to undo or to retrieve lost years. Despite professional success and pride in her children, life has had its ravages.

Leslie has had two marriages. Her first husband had been killed in the Korean War. She was left with two small children—two boys. This first marriage was too short, a love affair that has never been quieted. She married again: a tall, handsome man—his first marriage. " I knew from the beginning that there were serious problems. But he pursued me, and I guess I was both flattered and, perhaps, tired of searching. I had had a number of affairs, but no one of real interest. So here is this good-looking man, extremely gifted, and we shared the same political and intellectual views; so I succumbed and we married.

"He was a flirt, even during our courtship, but I tried to discount it. I thought I was overly sensitive, too jealous. It was a trait that I hated in myself. Flirting was harmless; it was not necessary to want to eradicate all other women. I tried to talk myself out of my awareness of the meaning of his behavior and my own recognition of my vulnerabilities. Unfortunately, reason did not work. He had a few affairs. I was distressed but strangely, I was so preoccupied with his audacious flirting that the affairs paled beside his everyday behavior. We could not go to a restaurant without his flirting with the waitress or walk down the street without his ogling every woman who passed. It was not done with a quick flicker of the eye, but with intense staring. There were other problems: anger, temperament, moodiness, all that probably could have been handled if I hadn't felt so betrayed by his yearnings after other women. I felt diminished in my eyes. He even tried to hit on my close friends. And that broke up the marriage. I left him. We had had a child, a lovely little girl. Divorce harmed her, as she loved her father. He had been inconsistent with my sons; they loved him and hated him. The conflict in this area was also overwhelming.

"Am I sad, yes? Perhaps if I had been stronger and less perturbed by his flirting, he would have outgrown it. I know it reflected his insecurity. I had established myself professionally, and he was struggling to develop a career while working on his doctorate.

"We remained friends; I knew that he loved me and did not want the divorce. After this marriage, I did not want another. I had many relationships, but never a deep love. There were casual affairs. I did not want to marry again until all the children were grown. Somehow I became too preoccupied with raising them, or maybe I was just gun-shy. I don't think I could have tolerated another womanizer in my life. One difficult marriage was enough. Yet there were men who were loyal and wanted to marry me. My regret: not to walk into old age with a gentle, loving partner.

Leslie speaks with dispassion, a quiet overview. But somewhere the betrayal still hurts, and has left an open wound. Why didn't this attractive woman remarry or find a meaningful long-term relationship? Why should the fear of betrayal play such a powerful role in her mental life? Are betrayals the ultimate definer of love between a couple? Is it not possible in the course of a long life to stray, to find another interesting for a brief time, and still love and desire one's partner? What is it that demands exclusiveness in our lives? Leslie asked these questions in our discussion. She had no answer either for me or for herself.

Case Six: BETTY

As I sit opposite Betty in a charming Mediterranean-style coffee shop, I observe a very attractive woman who in her youth had to have been very beautiful. In spite of silver-grey hair and the tell-tale wrinkles of age, her luminous eyes, and sly smile as she reveals her escapades, are evidence of a very adventurous woman. At eighty, she still volunteers in a school library, and in her younger days served in the Waves. She is a widow of many years and the mother of four sons. Betty was happily married for forty years and adored her husband. But this love did not preclude her from having a number of sexual affairs. Her husband, a surgeon, was tall, good-looking, and a very good lover. While sex was plentiful, she missed a certain feeling of passionate love.

She recounts with great delight the fact that on her trip to Switzerland she was the chosen one of all the women. The tour guide, a history professor, managed the *tête-à-tête* while the others were sleeping. This relationship lasted for a while. Her husband became suspicious when he found a letter from her lover, but this did not become problematic. Second and third affairs were less intense. To my question of any sense of remorse or guilt, she responded with some surprise and retorted: "Why should I?" She denied ever considering whether her husband had affairs until at one point in the interview. Betty suddenly reconsidered and wondered if at the many out-of-town conventions, he may have done so. There were times when he did not want her to accompany him. She soon left this thought and focused on her own delightful adulterous flings. Was it possible that her husband had affairs that she could not let herself acknowledge? Thus, her affairs during the marriage and subsequent affairs during her widowhood spared her the pain and distress of wounded pride. Better that she was the unfaithful one, the betrayer, and currently still the *femme fatale*!

Case Seven: STEPHEN

He came reluctantly to the interview. His wife had pushed him to see me. This reluctance pretty much described how Stephen approached life. He was of medium height and had sorrowful , brown eyes with a rather forlorn look. He was unhappy with his wife's sexual affairs, but could not get her to stop. He loved her dearly and never considered divorce. Not only did she sleep around promiscuously, but "forced" him to have affairs. He hated it, but slept with other women to please her. She would want to know the details, and even selected the women. If he refused, she would nag and withdraw from him. He did not enjoy the sex with other women, only sex with his wife.

It was a difficult interview, and I was reluctant to press with too many questions as I felt that this was a fragile man. I did wonder (to myself) if he unconsciously identified with his wife as she slept with other men, as though he was the woman having all these men in bed, a vicarious homosexual experience: something that he unconsciously wanted but did not dare act upon.

Case Nine: LEONARD

Leonard, a sixty-five year old man, has been in a relationship with his male partner for thirty-five years. It has been a tumultuous relationship with several separations, much turmoil and conflict. His partner, Eric, has been consistently unfaithful, and no longer denies his behavior or tries to change. In the early years of the relationship, Leonard fought hard against Eric's infidelities; there was much yelling, many emotional storms and crying, but now he accepts the reality that Eric cannot be faithful. He has never had another sexual or emotional relationship, nor does he wish to have one. He loves Eric dearly, and though, for the past five years they have had no sex, he is content to remain in the relationship; they are tied to one another and are good loving friends.

Here we observe an example of an intensive attachment by one person while the other requires multiple sexual relationships ranging from those that involve some intensity to one-night stands. Pain and pleasure go hand in hand, and life endures the cruelties of human nature.

Case Ten: JIM

Jim, handsome, tall, thin with an angular shaped face and large brown eyes, his discourse deceptively belies his twenty years. He has just completed his first year at Yale, has a keen intelligence, and a penetrating psychological awareness. And yet, there is some incongruity with the way he understands the social world of homosexuals and himself. His mannerisms, platinum-dyed hair, and dress already revealed a homosexual young man. Yet, when I asked to interview him, with a combustive force he blurted out, " I am gay." In the course of our interview, he could finally look inward and recognize that he is both rebellious and defensive about his sexuality. The fight is with the straight world and the homosexual world. The straight world does not easily accept homosexuality, and when he first came out as gay at the age of 16, many boys who had been his friends at school withdrew from the friendship. In the homosexual world bisexuality is frowned upon. "You are either straight or gay, no in-between." Perhaps what is most distressing is the quality of relationships. It is easy to go to bed, to have sex, but to find someone "you feel connected to, who has a sense of who you are or dares to challenge you in a meaningful way, is hard to find." Jim has many friends, and he has had three important relationships since he came out, but nothing to meet his deeper emotional needs. He feels especially close to two female friends; these are non-sexual relationships, but he has not been able to achieve this with a gay man. Despite his general affect of gaiety and easy laughter, there is a sense of sadness about him. There is a lot of sex to be had, but little of the intimacy and closeness that he would want.

He related a recent incident of meeting a gay married couple at a party where he observed the husband go off with another man to have sex. It was obvious to him that the abandoned husband was very unhappy. The question can be easily raised as to whether the problem of closeness and intimacy rests with Jim, his internal conflicts, his fears of an unfaithful lover, or whether the problem reflects a society that encourages sex without intimacy, a superficiality in relationships?

Prior to Jim's full acknowledgement that he was gay, he dated girls, and had his first sexual experience at age fourteen. Sex was pretty accessible at his high school, a small suburb outside of Chicago. He had oral sex, there was no difficulty in getting a 'blow job' from his girlfriend, but he was unable to perform in intercourse. He could not get an erection. Hook-ups were quite common. There was a lot of peer pressure to have sex; for guys it was to prove you were cool, and for girls it was a way of getting guys, to be wanted and popular. Girls felt obligated to have sex, as if they owed the guy something "if he took you out on a date." If you wanted to be the "topic of conversation," you had to be sexual. Kids were more concerned with their bodies than learning about themselves, and " all we talked about was sex." Sexting was a big occupation, and he, too, sent pictures of himself displaying his penis. The girls sent full-body pictures of their nudity while the boys just displayed their penises. Essentially, the gay world does not differ from the straight world of his high-school days.

Case 11: ALLAN

Allan is a sixty-year old man, tall, attractive with Nordic looks, and pepper-gray hair, somewhat spiked in a modish style.

He spoke rapidly on many subjects, appeared interested in psychoanalysis and questioned how it helped people. He was quite intelligent, liked to read, but explained that he had not finished high school He loved music and played the trumpet, though not professionally. The family owned a chain of grocery stores and he helped to operate the business. In his early years, he was quite rebellious and fought with his father. He regrets the path that he took in youth when he had been in a few detention homes.

Though he answered my request to discuss infidelity and betrayal, it was clear that this was not easy for him. "Oh, yes," he said when I gently moved the subject back to betrayal, "I don't feel good about it. I fooled around when I was married." He married at age 21 a woman a year his junior, with whom he had been living. Even prior to the marriage, he was fooling around, never intercourse but heavy kissing and petting. His wife suspected, as she walked in when he had another woman in their apartment. This occurred prior to the marriage, but she still wanted to marry him. He loved her but could not stop himself from his attraction to other women. Sex with his wife was good at the beginning, but then he became bored. His wife finally left him after five years of marriage. They continue to be good friends, and are in frequent contact. She is living on the West coast and at times he considers moving there. He dates other women, but no real interest in any sustained relationship.

Allan seems on the surface happy, but there is a restless quality to his movements and the rapidity of his speech reveals a sense of a rapidly-moving man as though he is running from somewhere to nowhere.

Case 12: DONALD

Donald, an eighty-year-old man, had heard of my work from a friend and approached me. He was interested in telling his story. Perhaps, age and memories drove the impulse to recount the pleasures of bygone days. He had been married for thirty years; his wife died twenty years ago. He had many affairs during his marriage, which he described as a difficult relationship. His wife lost interest in sex early in the marriage: "She was not a good lover anyway." He had many one-night stands that were sexually satisfying. His work as a businessman required travel; thus, it made it easy to have unencumbered sex—no ties. He does enjoy sex and "loves a woman's body." There have been a few long-term relationships, but nothing of any significance that would have made him consider leaving his wife. They had three children, and his wife was totally absorbed with raising them. He has a close relationship with two of his daughters and a so-so rapport with his son. Donald had been involved with a slightly older woman for the past two years who would like to live with him. He prefers his freedom, and they spend weekends together, which meets his needs. He has been faithful to her, but indicated that if any woman reached out to him, he could be tempted to have sex with her.

Interesting that though the marriage was not a good one from the perspective of understanding and closeness, and, furthermore, the sex was only intermittent, Donald had no thought of leaving the marriage. He expressed neither guilt nor remorse. Rather, he enjoyed the various sexual encounters; life was interesting.

These interviews were an attempt to demonstrate the multiple reactions to betrayal. We observe deep pain, rage, fear of further emotional involvement, contradictory behavior, bordering on hypocrisy, lack of self awareness, and denial of reality. To suffer infidelity or to be the adulterer is never an easy path to travel and is strewn with thorns among the roses.

.

Conclusion

To hear the sexual words and bawdy encounters in Shakespeare is to be met with parody and irony, and introduces us to humanity's struggles over power, its vices and wars, and battles between the sexes. To encounter sexual words and human interaction in movies and TV in the twenty-first century is to be left with a lascivious taste in one's mouth, and a quiescent mentation stimulated by the allure of sexualized bodies. As Lillian Rubin (1990) queried in her book *Erotic Wars*: what is happening to relationships, that mode of interchange among people where regard and concern ought to dominate the interaction, and not the wish to seduce and conquer? Certainly, sexual freedom has been attained, and, unleashed from the hypocrisy of the Victorian Era. Seemingly, sexual relations would seem to have attained an atmosphere of frankness that would encompass kindness and gentleness, especially among the sexes. Unfortunately, as we have revealed by our examination of the cultural atmosphere of this era, the sexting, hook-ups and the social interaction, we are confronted by pressured sex, nasty epithets, and mental cruelty, especially among the young.

The single adult population appears to be paying their tithes to loneliness, and despair, along with destructive behavior to both self and other (Rogers and Whelihan, 2012; Bushnell, 1998). We would not have anticipated that sex, that instinctual drive that has the capacity to develop into love and attachment, would have gone astray in this twenty-first century. But unfortunately the freedom and pleasures that we hoped for have been short-lived, for we are also dependent on culture that has the capacity to define and set pathways for the manner in which the sexual drive is expressed. Culture, further, helps determine the ideologies that govern in-dividual behavior and value systems. The mixture of culture and biology gives rise in our mental apparatus to a psychology of the mind. Sexual freedom, ungoverned by society, does not have the capacity to provide for ultimate happiness or an inner sense of stasis. Without a social order that recognizes and institutes rules of behavior that can care for and protect both individuals and society, we are at the behest of raw emotions, the instincts that require taming and modulation. We are also at the mercy of culture that when controlled by forces more concerned with wealth and power, can result in destructive behaviors for the individual and ultimately for the entire society.

Perhaps, we are in a transition period, and so we must give the beginning of this century the benefit of doubt. But the forebodings do not look good. The rate of divorce is high, adultery appears to be climbing; one cannot really speak of infidelity in dating or cohabitation, since the rule of engagement is loose. The numbers of unmarried are increasing, family ties and relationships are impaired, and thus we have a lonely and unsupported population. Add to this the number of children in one-parent families, single mothers, and a society that has not met the needs of children adequately. Poverty and economic stress may appear as a result of the decline of marriage and monogamy, or at least are an associated cause. Yet, more precisely, we need to claim that the break-up of marriages and the highly sexualized climate are more related to economic and political factors that dominate society. Are we really free-spirited, unhampered by social mores in our sexual lives, or are we unknown prisoners of a sexuality deprived of real love and concern, a consumerization of sex and body?

Bibliography

AARP Research Study, 07/01/2015.

Abbott, E. (2010). *Mistresses: The History of Other Women.* New York: Overlook Press,

Abbott, K. (2009). *Sin in the Second City.* New York: Random House.

Albert, A. (2001). *Brothel. Mustang Ranch and Its Women.* New York: Random House.

Anonymous. *The Nunnery Tales.*

Aries, P. (1960). *Centuries Of Childhood.* New York: Vintage Books,

Bader, M. (2002). *Arousal: the Secret Logic of Sexual Fantasies.* New York: Thomas Dunne Books, St Martin's Press

Beshorov and West. (1998) Census Bureau Population Survey.

Billieon, M. & Ray, J., (2012). *Death of the Cheating Man: What Every Woman Must Know About Men Who Stray.* New York: Strebor Books.

Bogin, M. (1976). *The Women Troubadours.* New York and London Paddington: Press Ltd.

Boteach, S. (2014). *Kosher Lust.* Jerusalem and New York: Gefen Publishing House,

Brookover, L. (1989). *Defining Rape.* Durham: Duke University Press.

Brumberg, J. (1997). *The Body Project.* New York: Random House.

Bushnell, C. (1989). *Sex and the City.* New York: Grand Central Publishing-Hachette book Group.

Califia, P. (1994). *Public Sex: The Culture of Radical Sex.* Jersey City: Cleis Press.

Chaucer, G. (2013). *The Canterbury Tales: A New an Unabridged Translation by Burton Raffel.* New York. The Modern Library:

Cherlin, A. (2010). *The Marriage-Go-Round.* New York: Random House.

——— (2012). *Public and Private Families.* New York: Random

House.

Cleland, J. (1897). *The Life and Adventures of Fanny Hill*. London: Oxford University Press.

Cohen, K. (2011). *Dirty Little Secrets: Breaking The Silence On Teenage Girls and Promiscuity,* Naperville, Il: Source Books.

Coontz, S. (2005). *Marriage a History: From Obedience to Intimacy, or How Love Conquered Marriage.* New York: Viking Penguin,

Darwin, Charles C. (1859). *On the Origin of Species by Means of Natural Selection or The Preservation of Favored Races and the Struggle for Life.* John Murray: London.

Dawkins, R. (2006). *The Selfish Gene.* New York: Oxford University Press.

de Sade, Marquis (1968). *One Hundred Days Of Sodom.* New York: Grove Press.

Easton, D. & Hardy, J.W. (2009 [1997]). *The Ethical Slut: A Practical Guide to Polyamory, Open Relationships & Other Adventures.* Berkeley, CA: Celestial Arts.

Eissler, R.K. (1959). On Isolation. *Psychoanalytic Study of the Child* 14:29–60.

Escoffier, J. ed. (2003). Sexual Revolution. New York. Thunder's Mouth Press:

Freedman, P. (1999). *Images of the Medieval Peasant.* Stanford: Stanford University Press.

Fisher, H. (1992). *Anatomy of Love.* New York: W.W. Norton & Co.

——— (2004). *Why We Love: The Nature and Chemistry of Romantic Love.* New York: Holt Paperbacks.

Flanders, J. (2003). *The Victorian House: Domestic Life from Childbirth to Deathbed.* New York: Thomas Dunne Books, St. Martin's Press.

Flaubert, G. (1821). *Madame Bovary.* London: Penguin Classicsm, 2001.

Foucault, M. (1978). *The History of Sexuality.* New York: Random House, 1990.

Frankel, E. Northwestern University Gender and Sexualities Resource Center.

Freud, S. (1915). Instincts and Their Vicissitudes. *Standard Edition* 14.

——— (1927). Civilization and Its Discontents. *Standard Edition* 21.

Galenson, E. & Roiphe, H. (1981*). Infantile Origins of Sexual Identity.* New York: International Universities Press.

Gallup Poll (2013).

Gracie, X. (2015). *Wide Open: A Memoir.* Oakland, CA. New Harbinger Publications.

Hardy. T. (1891 [2012]). *Tess of the dur'Bervilles.* London: Penguin Classics.

Hastings, A. S. (1996 [1851]). *Body and Soul: Sexuality on the Brink of Change.* Boston: Da Capo Press.

Hawthorne, N. (1850 [2017]). *The Scarlet Letter.* Charleston, SC: CreateSpace Independent Publishing Platform.

Herlihy, D. (1985). *Medieval Households.* Cambridge, MA & London: Harvard Press.

Hills. R. (2015). *The Sex Myth: The Gap Between Fantasy and Reality.* New York: Simon and Schuster Paperbacks.

Houston, R. (2002). *Is He Cheating On You? 829 Telltale Signs.* Kansas City, MO: Lifestyle Publication. (www.InfidelityAdvise.com).

Hughes, K. (1998). *Every Day Life in Regency and Victorian England.* Fort Collins: Writer's Digest Books.

Hurst, J.G. (1961). *The Medieval Peasant House,* ed. A. Smart. Edinburgh: Fourth Viking Congress.

Jackson, A. (2004). *The History of Prostitution Reform in the United States.* Knoxville: University of Tennessee Honors Program.

Katz, J.N. (1978). *Gay American History.* New York: Avon Books.

Kern, L. & Malone, N. (2015). *The Sex Myth.* New York Magazine.

Kidder, R. (2013) Morals and Technology. in Sexting, ed. Scherer Gale Press

Kimmel, M. (2008). *Guyland.* New York: Harper Collins,

Kinsey, A., Pomeroy, W. S., & Martin, C. E. (1948). *Sexual Behavior in the Human Male.* Philadelphia: Saunders.

Klein, Marty (2012). When children See Internet Pornography. The New York Times, May 9, 2012.

Klinenberg, E. (2012). *Going Solo.* New York: The Penguin Press,

Krasnow, I. (2014). *Sex After . . . Women Share How Intimacy Changes as Life Changes.* New York: Gotham.

Lindsay, J. (1976). *The Troubadours and their World.* London: Frederick Muller Limited.

Livnat, A.I., Papadimitriou, C., Dushoff, J, , & Feldman, M.W. (2008). A mixability theory for the role of sex in evolution. *Proceedings of the National Academy of Sciences* 105(50):19803–19808.

Lovejoy, C.O. The Origin of Man. *Science, New Series,* 211(4480): 341–350.

Lukas, D. & Clutton-Brock, T.H. (2013). The Evolution of Social Monogamy in Mammals. *Science* 341(6145): 526–530.

March, A. (2011). *Romancing the Countess.* New York: Penguin Group.

Mead, M., (1949). *Male and Female: A Study of Sexes in a Changing World.* New York: William Morrow.

Millot, M. (2015). *The School Of Venus, Or The Ladies Delight: Reduced Into Rules Of Practice: Being The Translation Of The French L'Escoles Des Filles.* London: Locus Elm Press.

Mitchell, S. (1996). *Daily Life In Victorian England.* Westport and London: The Greenwood Press.

Mosher, C.D., (2011) . Sex in the Victorian Age. In: Crooks and Baur, eds. *Our Sexuality.* Belmont, CA: Wadsworth.

Murphy K. (2011) . *By Gone Days.* New York: Coachlight Press, Fictional Magazine,

Millott, M. (2017). The School of Venus. Lebanon, IN : Samson Family Leather.

Myers, J. (2012). *Hooked Up.* Stamford, CT: York House Press

Orenstein, P. (2016). *Girls and Sex.* New York: Harper Collins.

Pew Research, 2009, 2011, 2013, 2014.

Picard, L. (2005). *Victorian London.* New York: St. Martin's Press.

Ponton, L. (2000). *The Sex Lives of Teenagers.* New York: Dutton.

Price, H. & Watts, J. (2007). *Power and Identity in the Middle Ages: Essays in Memory of Rees Davis.* Oxford Scholarship Online. Oct 2011, University Press Online.

Ridley, M. (1993). The *Red Queen: Sex And The Evolution of Human Nature.* London: Viking.

Robertson, Stephen, (Feb. 2016) . "Age of Consent Laws in Children and Youth in History," Item # 230/ case studies.

Rodgers, A. & Whelihan, M. (2012). Kiss and Tell. Soft Spot Press.

Rose, C. (2004) *Longing To Tell: Black Women Talk About Sexuality and Intimacy.* New York: Farrar, Straus and Giroux:

Ryan, C. and Jetha, C. (2010). *Sex at Dawn.* New York and London. Harper Perennial.

Rubin, L.B. (1990). *Erotic Wars.* New York: Farrar, Straus & Giroux.

Sacher-Masoch, Ritter Von, (2000 [1870]). *Venus In Furs.* New York: Penguin Group.

Scheidel, W. (2008). Monogamy and Polygyny in Greece, Roman and World History. Version 1.0. Stanford University.

Scherer, L.S, ed. (2013). *Sexting.* US and London: Gale Press, Greengage Learning.

Schwendinger & Schwendinger (1985).

Shahar, S. (1990). *Childhood in The Middle Ages.* London and New York: Routledge.

Sheehy, G. (2006). *Sex and the Seasoned Woman.* New York, Random House.

Sheff, E. (2004). What Polyamory Is and What It Is Not. *Psychology Today*, Sept. 9.

Shields, W.M. & Shields, L.M. (1982). What Causes Rape? A

dissenting view, Science, 82, 3, 16.

Smart, C. (1995). *Has Adultery Become a Spurious Issue?* on the Independent website on May 22, 1995.

Smith, I. (2012). *The Truth About Men.* New York: St. Martins Press.

Stark, E. (1985, February). The psychological aftermath. *Psychology Today* 48.

Stolorow, R.D. & Brandchaft, B. (1987). Developmental Failure and Psychic Conflict. *Psychoanalytic Psychology* 4(3):241–253.

Schwendinger, J.S. & Schwendinger, H. (1985) Homo Economics as the Rapist. In *Violence against Women: A Critique of the Sociobiology of Rape* by Suzanne R. Sunday and Ethel Tobach. New York: Gordian Press.

Tavernise, S. (2011). National Marriage and Divorce Rate, Trends. Center For Disease Control.

Tennyson, A.L. (1900). *The Princess: A Medley.* Glenview, IL Scott, Foresman and Co.

Thiessen, D. (1983) Rape as a reproductive strategy: Our evolutionary analysis. Paper presented at the American Psychological Association Meeting, Los Angeles, CA.

Thornhill, R. & Thornhill, N.W (1983). Human rape: An evolutionary analysis *Ethology and Sociobiology* 4:137–173.

Tolstoy, L. (2018 [1877]). *Anna Karenina,* transl. C. Garnett. Charleston, SC: CreateSpace Independent Publishing Platform.

Tuchman, B. (1987). *A Distant Mirror: The Calamitous 14th Century.* New York: Random House.

Vygotsky, L.S. (1954). *Thought and Language.* Cambridge: MIT Press, 198Got .

Waite, L.J., Browning, D., Doherty, W.J., Gallagher, M., Yee, L., & Stanley, S.M. (2002). *Does Divorce Make People Happy?* New York: Institute For American Values.

Waite, L.J. & Gallagher, M. (2000). *The Case for Marriage: Why Married People are Happier, Healthier, and Better Off Financially.* New York: Doubleday.

Walker, A. (1866). A Poem. In: S. Mitchell, *Daily Life in Victorian England*. Westport: Greenwood, 1996.

—— (2004) *What About the Kids? Raising Your Children Before, During, and After Divorce*. New York: Hachette Book Group.

Wikipedia, the Free Encyclopedia (2007). *History of Human Sexuality*.

Wikipedia, the Free Encyclopedia (2014). *Hunter-Gatherer*.

Wikipedia, the Free Encyclopedia, (2018). *Middle Ages*.

Wikipedia, the Free Encyclopedia (2007). *The Invisible Sex*.

Wilson, C. (1998). *A Study Of Sexual Disorders: The Misfits*. New York: Carroll & Graf Publishers.

Yalom, M. (2001) *A History of the Wife*. New York: HarperCollins.

www.ingramcontent.com/pod-product-compliance
Lightning Source LLC
Chambersburg PA
CBHW071232020426
42333CB00015B/1445